THE ESSENTIAL MOSIMANN

THE ESSENTIAL
MOSIMANN

Anton Mosimann with Tiffany Daneff

EBURY PRESS LONDON

**To all those in this wonderful profession
who inspired me over the years and taught me to
enjoy the quality of life**

First published 1993

1 3 5 7 9 10 8 6 4 2

Text and Recipes © Anton Mosimann 1993
Photographs © Ebury Press 1993

Anton Mosimann has asserted his right under the
Copyright, Designs and Patents Act, 1988 to be
identified as the author of this work.

First published in the United Kingdom in 1993 by
Ebury Press
Random House, 20 Vauxhall Bridge Road, London
SW1V 2SA

Random House Australia (Pty) Limited
20 Alfred Street, Milsons Point, Sydney,
New South Wales 2061, Australia

Random House New Zealand Limited
18 Poland Road, Glenfield
Auckland 10, New Zealand

Random House South Africa (Pty) Limited
PO Box 337, Bergvlei, South Africa

Random House UK Limited Reg. No. 954009

A CIP catalogue record for this book is available from
the British Library

ISBN 0 09 175379 1

Recipe and Text Editor: **Susan Fleming**

Designer: **Clive Hayball**

Reportage Photography: **Nic Barlow**

Food Photography: **James Murphy**

Food Stylist: **Kit Chan**

Typeset in Helvetica by Textype Typesetters,
Cambridge

Colour separations by Magnacraft, London

Printed and bound in Italy by New Interlitho S.p.a., Milan

Papers used by Ebury Press are natural, recyclable
products made from wood grown in sustainable forests.

Contents

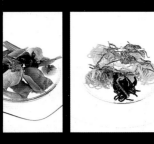

Foreword

As everybody who knows nothing about it knows the Swiss are stolid, dull and solvent. None of this was ever entirely true. Now practically all of it is mistaken. It would be truer to say that the swiss are anxious, introspective and threatened. This state of affairs has had the side effect of provoking their imagination in a way which has never really been necessary before. Although it is often forgotten that Switzerland is not only the producer of the world's most sophisticated timepieces and the most delectable chocolates, but also of the most auspicious and hilarious clowns.

It is certainly these qualities of precision, of refinement and of fantasy which lie behind the success of one of the country's most distinguished culinary ambassadors, Anton Mosimann. he is not only an outstanding *Chef de cuisine* but an arbiter of taste, a creator of ambience.

His celebrated restaurant is situated in the leafy serenity between Knightsbridge and Eaton Square, in a deconsecrated church. This building, treated with extraordinary vision, is a microcosm of Switzerland itself, being a place of high, jagged peaks with splendid food in the cosiness of the valleys. Concealed high in its Elysium are four lovely rooms for private parties and a bar.

THE MENU IS PROOF OF ANTON MOSIMANN'S GREAT ORIGINALITY. THE CUISINE IS NEITHER 'TRADITIONAL' NOR 'NOUVELLE', NOR IS IT ENSLAVED BY A NEO-JAPANESE OF MINIMILISM, BUT IS UNIQUELY MOSIMANN. IT IS SOMEWHAT IRONIC THAT THIS SWISS CHEF TOOK THE HUMDRUM BRITISH CUISINE AND MADE IT HAUTE COUTURE – HIS BREAD AND BUTTER PUDDING AND HUMBLE FISH CAKE ARE NOW EATEN BY THE CROWN HEADS OF EUROPE. NOT THE LEAST OF HIS TRIUMPHS IS A CHRISTMAS PUDDING WHICH APPEARS SEASONALLY ON THE SHELVES IN IT'S SMART BLACK BOX WITH THE RED 'M' EMBLAZONED ON IT. AND NOT ONLY HAS HE TAKEN ON THE FOOD OF HIS ADOPTED LAND, BUT ALL THOSE COUNTRIES THAT HE HAD THE GOOD FORTUNE TO PASS THROUGH; HIS RISOTTO ENJOYS A CONSIDERABLE REPUTATION IN ROME AND THAT IS QUITE AN ACHIEVEMENT, WHICH TOGETHER WITH MEMORIES OF MEALS ENJOYED UNDER THE SPIRE, MAKES ANYONE WITH ANY SENSIBILITY WISH TO FIND OUT MORE ABOUT THE ESSENTIAL MOSIMANN. I WILL THEREFORE EMULATE ANTON'S ADMIRABLE SENSE OF PROPORTION AND ALLOW HIM TO SPEAK FOR HIMSELF.

SIR PETER USTINOV

Chapter One

Early Days

I CAN STILL REMEMBER, AS CLEARLY AS IF IT WERE ONLY YESTERDAY THE SWEET SMELL OF DARK, SUGARED FRUIT BUBBLING IN THE HEAVY COPPER PRESERVING PAN. MY MOTHER LOVED MAKING JAMS AND JELLIES AND ON THESE DAYS THE FRAGRANCE WOULD FILL THE WHOLE HOUSE, MOVING IN A WARM, FRUITY AND SWEET STEAM FROM THE RESTAURANT'S KITCHEN TO OUR FLAT UPSTAIRS.

FROM MY BEDROOM I COULD SEE OVER THE RED-TILED ROOFTOPS OF OUR VILLAGE TO THE OUTLINE OF DARK FIRS IN THE FOOTHILLS OF THE HIGH JURA. WE HAD MOVED HERE, TO A RESTAURANT IN THE VILLAGE OF NIDAU, NEAR BIEL, WHICH IS IN THE CANTON OF BERNE, WHEN I WAS FIVE YEARS OLD.

BEFORE THAT WE HAD LIVED IN THE SMALL TOWN OF GRENCHEN WHERE MY PARENTS RAN A FARM AS WELL AS A RESTAURANT. THOUGH I CAN REMEMBER LITTLE FROM THOSE EARLY YEARS, WHAT EMERGES MOSTLY FROM THOSE HAZY SHADOWS ARE THE MOMENTS ON THE FARM WHEN I HELPED TO COLLECT EGGS FROM THE HENS OR WATCHED AS THE FARM-HAND MILKED THE COWS. WE HAD HORSES AND SHEEP AS WELL AS A NUMBER OF RABBITS WHICH I FED AND WATERED.

BOTH MY PARENTS COOKED, THOUGH MY FATHER PREFERRED TO MAKE THE MEAT AND SAUCE DISHES, AND I BECAME USED TO SEEING THEM ALWAYS BUSY EITHER INSIDE AT THE

I'm about five years old here, with Berni, my much loved dog. He would sleep in my room, and follow me as I skied to school. He would also be waiting there for me at the end of the day – how he knew the time, I don't know! When he died, aged about fifteen, I felt I'd lost my best friend.

stove, or outside tending the animals or picking fruit and vegetables for the restaurant. Whatever the season, there was always work to be done.

I was an only child and quite lonely. As my parents were working I tended to stay at home a lot which made it difficult to make friends with other children outside school. I made friends instead with the people around me, like the young men and women who helped out in the restaurant, and with my parents' friends.

Our home was the restaurant. We didn't even have a kitchen upstairs and hardly ever used our own sitting-room, but preferred to gather together in the restaurant where friends were always welcome. I grew used to the fact that we were rarely alone as a family, even at Christmas when my father would invite those without families of their own to share our food. Though that meant sometimes eating with complete strangers, we were always happy, and I think that made me aware very early in life how much pleasure a good meal can give.

Since my parents stayed up late every night, clearing the restaurant, I used to get my own breakfast before walking the two long miles to school and back. In winter, when the snow lay thick, I sometimes skied to school. Like all the other children, I had been put on skis when I

THE BAKER WOULD BE UP BY THREE OR FOUR O'CLOCK IN THE MORNIN

HE WORKED INSTINCTIVELY AND I USED TO WATCH, FASCINATED, AS HE PULL

A KNIFE TO GIVE IT A DISTINCTIVE CRISS-CROSS PATTER

was only three and it quickly became second nature. In the afternoon the great treat was to catch the bus up the hill back home to be greeted by the welcoming glow of the yellow light shining from the restaurant windows.

I did well at school, and received a lot of encouragement and kindness from my teacher, Erwin Allemann, now in his eighties. He was a great friend and taught me a good deal more about life than just the three 'Rs'. Even today we keep in touch, and I go and visit him whenever I'm in Switzerland.

In the evenings I used to sit in the warm restaurant on a carved wooden chair with my homework spread out over one of the tables while my parents were busy in the kitchen, chopping vegetables and preparing sauces. They were good cooks. They made simple food, nothing fine but good, honest cuisine; lots of pasta dishes which my father loved, braises of beef and veal, rabbit, roasts, *sauerkraut* and cheese fondue. When I had finished my homework, I would help wherever I could, chopping herbs, putting baskets of fresh bread on the tables, or doing the washing up. Sometimes, though, I couldn't wait to help in the kitchen, so the homework would be folded up and put away until the next morning when I had to be up very early to get it finished in time.

My parents didn't bake their own bread as the baker lived next door, and the bread would arrive still warm from the oven each morning. One of my favourite pastimes was helping him fetch and chop firewood to stoke the clay oven. As I worked my face became flushed with the heat from the glowing embers. I thought that was hot, but it was nothing compared to the oil-fired stoves I later worked on in the kitchens of some old hotels.

The baker would be up by three or four o'clock in the morning, working the heavy slabs of dough with his large floury hands. He made a sweet milk bread called *Zopf* as well as ordinary brown and white farmhouse loaves. He worked instinctively and I used to watch, fascinated, as he pulled and patted the dough into shape and then cut the top with a knife to give it a distinctive criss-cross pattern.

That was a long time ago, but I can still smell that wonderful scent of freshly baked bread as he pulled the hot loaves out of the oven. I make *Zopf* and other bread at home even now, but I like to ring the changes, using different grains and flours, or including ingredients such as onions or walnuts and raisins. The green olive bread on page 16 is a new favourite.

Growing up in those circumstances, I think it would have been difficult not to have learnt to love food. My par- >

. . .)RKING THE HEAVY SLABS OF DOUGH WITH HIS LARGE FLOURY HANDS . . .

'D PATTED THE DOUGH INTO SHAPE AND THEN CUT THE TOP WITH

We didn't make our own bread at the restaurant in Nidau, as the baker, Albert Gnägi, lived right next door. Albert was one of my closest friends when I was very young, and many is the time I got up at around 4 a.m. to help him chop the wood, and light the fires to get the clay oven hot, ready for baking.

11

A GREAT LESSON I LEARNED AT AN EARLY AGE

WAS HOW TO SET ONESELF A GOAL TO WORK TOWARDS.

MOST OF THE THINGS I HAVE GAINED IN LIFE, I HAVE

ACHIEVED THROUGH DETERMINATION, PERSEVERANCE AND PATIENCE.

ents' interest and enthusiasm were more than infectious, they must have been absorbed directly into my blood-stream. There were always fresh herbs in the house and gleaming rows of home-made preserves in the larder. My mother used whatever berries or fruits were in season to make all kinds of jams and jellies: rhubarb with strawberry, bilberry, rich plum, pale golden quince jelly, and my favourite, black cherry jam, each glowing pot covered with a neat square of colourful cloth. She also used fruit a lot in simple dishes which could be eaten as either desserts or breakfast – the following poached pears, for instance.

On my days off from school I loved to see the fresh fish and meat arriving daily and would watch as my father selected the choice cuts. They waited until they had seen the meat and then decided on which dishes to prepare, something I have always believed to be important.

Spending a lot of time in the kitchen, as I did, I learnt all the basic techniques, how to crack and beat eggs, the way to make a *roux*, how much seasoning to add or, sim-ply, how to tell when food is cooked. I do believe children >

Poached Pears

SERVES 4

4 large pears (Comice are good)	Core and peel carefully, leaving the stems on if possible.
600 ml (1 pint) water 100 g (4 oz) sugar, or to taste ½ cinnamon stick 1 vanilla pod rind and juice of 1 lemon (optional)	Heat together in a pan large enough to hold the pears standing upright. Place the pears in the pan, stems up. They should be completely covered by the syrup. Poach them at just below boiling point until soft, about 10–12 minutes, depending on ripeness. Remove the pears, and reduce the syrup until fairly thick. Cool. When the pears and syrup are cold, place in a serving dish, or in a container in which they will keep (in the fridge) for a day or two.
4 sprigs fresh mint icing sugar	Garnish each individual plate with a mint sprig, and dust with icing sugar.

ANTON'S TIP

Serve as a compote for breakfast, with yoghurt perhaps, or as a dessert with some chocolate ice cream (see page 85).

On the right, Lucien Cornu, chef at the Baeren Hotel in Twann, where I worked for 2½ years. He taught me the basics of cooking.

should be encouraged into the kitchen to learn about food when they are young. That way they get a feel for the texture of raw and cooked food, and gain a sense of what flavours complement each other and what combinations will or won't work. Obviously not all of them will become chefs, but at least they'll know how to make themselves supper or a snack without relying on pre-cooked meals.

It was very early on, perhaps when aged seven or eight, that I decided to be a cook when I grew up. I suppose boys usually dream of becoming a racing driver or a pilot or something glamorous, but I always wanted to be a cook, somebody who worked in the kitchen, essentially because I loved handling food.

I inherited that from my mother, who was passionate about food. Sometimes as a treat after school she would take me to a *pâtisserie* for tea and her favourite strawberry *gâteau*.

'You are never too young,' she used to say, 'to learn >

Herb-Steamed Poussins

SERVES 4

4 poussins, about 400 g (14 oz) each ½ garlic clove, peeled 40 g (1½ oz) soft butter	Rub the poussins all over with the garlic, then brush with the butter.
1 bunch coriander, leaves shredded, stems reserved	Very gently loosen the skin covering the breasts and insert the coriander leaves.
salt and freshly ground pepper 40 g (1½ oz) bear garlic leaves (see Tip)	Season the poussins lightly, and wrap in the leaves. Line a steaming basket with foil and place the poussins in it.
1 small piece fresh root ginger, peeled and cut into small strips	Sprinkle over the poussins and set aside.
1 litre (1¾ pints) White Poultry Stock (see page 156) juice of 1 lemon 2 shallots, peeled and sliced	In the base of the steamer bring to the boil together, along with the coriander stalks. Continue to boil until reduced to 600 ml (1 pint). Place the steamer basket on top, cover and simmer for about 15 minutes.
½ cucumber, peeled, seeded and sliced 2 tomatoes, quartered and seeded	Add to the steamer and continue to cook for a further 3–5 minutes until the poussins are tender and the vegetables cooked.
4 sprigs flat-leaved parsley or coriander	Garnish with herbs. Serve some of the stock as a sauce to accompany the poussins.

ANTON'S TIP

Bear garlic – *Allium ursinum* or ramsons – is a member of the lily family to which leeks, onions and garlic belong, and is quite widespread in the wild in Europe. The smell is powerfully garlicky, but it diminishes on cooking.

Green Olive Bread

SERVES 4   OVEN: Moderately hot, 200°C/400°F/Gas 6

500 g (18 oz) wholewheat flour	Place in a warmed bowl, and make a well in the centre.
40 g (1½ oz) fresh yeast, or 20 g (¾ oz) dried a pinch of sugar 250 ml (8 fl oz) lukewarm water	Dissolve the yeast with the pinch of sugar in a little of the lukewarm water. Pour into the well in the flour.
40 ml (1½ fl oz) cold-pressed virgin olive oil 10 g (⅓ oz) salt	Add half the oil, the salt and the remaining water to the well in the flour and mix all together well. Knead on a lightly floured surface to form a pliable smooth dough. This will take about 5–10 minutes. Place the dough in a warmed bowl, cover and leave to rise in a warm place until it has doubled in size, about 30–60 minutes. Knock the dough back by kneading briefly again – about 5 minutes – then return to the bowl, cover, leave to rise again for 20–30 minutes.
100 g (4 oz) pitted green olives, halved 20 ml (2 dessertspoons) each of finely cut fresh dill, lemon balm and marjoram	Squeeze, very carefully and thoroughly, all the moisture from the olives. Mix with the chopped herbs. Turn the dough out on to a board and knead the green mixture into the dough. Form into a cob shape and place on an oiled baking sheet. Brush with the remaining olive oil and sprinkle the top with some extra wholewheat flour. Cover loosely and leave to rise once more for 10 minutes. Bake in the preheated oven for 20 minutes then turn the oven down to 180°C/350°F/Gas 4, and bake for a further 25 minutes. The bread is ready when the base sounds hollow on tapping it with the knuckles. Put on a wire rack to cool.

ANTON'S TIP

It is important to squeeze the olives as dry as possible, otherwise the bread can be heavy. Good olives to use are those from Mallorca because of their nutty flavour.

how these things taste!'

Another of her favourite dishes was roast *poussin*, baby chicken, and in the school holidays whenever I was at home she would take me out on Monday, the day the restaurant was closed, to a restaurant about fifteen miles away which served a particularly delicious *poussin*. They cooked it with wild herbs gathered from the surrounding pastures, but I have since adapted the recipe, steaming the birds rather than roasting them, which is more healthy.

I loved those trips and the food as well, of course, but by the time I was eight, instead of accompanying my parents on their day out, I had opted to stay at home and cook. It was my chance to use the kitchen and I would spend the day preparing dinner for my friends from the village. I liked to experiment with food like a chemist in his laboratory. Rather than use a recipe book, I would embellish or adapt basic recipes learnt from my mother.

Pasta was one of my favourite meals and I loved making different sauces. These were usually meat-based with tomatoes and fresh herbs, but each week I varied the quantities and ingredients. We had a kitchen garden where we grew herbs and I would pick leaves of basil, tarragon, parsley and oregano for the sauces. Even as a boy I loved spicy food, so I sometimes sprinkled on cayenne or added a few chillies to my dishes. Once I added rather too much mustard to a cheese fondue but we ate it all up anyway. I learnt from an early age that there is nothing more satisfying for a chef than seeing a stack of empty plates after a good meal.

Other early favourites were *Wurstsalat, sausage salad*, and *Rösti*, a Swiss dish of fried grated potatoes with bacon and onions. Today I still make *Rösti*, but I have adapted the recipe, sometimes leaving out the bacon and onion, and topping it with a quail's egg and caviar, or mix-

ing some apple into the basic potato mix and topping it with grilled goats' cheese.

The other great lesson I learnt at an early age was how to set oneself a goal to work towards. Most of the things I have gained in life, I have achieved through determination, perseverance and patience. Luck helps, but you never know when it'll turn up.

I'll never forget one particular day. Walking through the village on some errand or other, my eyes were drawn to an incredible car parked outside a shop. It was a light blue Chevrolet Corvair, and quite beautiful. I walked all the way round it, and as I peered inside at the luxurious upholstery and gleaming chrome, I knew that one day I had to have a car like that myself. Once I set my mind on something, I rarely give it up and all the way home I tried to think of ways of making money. I was determined that by the time I was eighteen, I would be able to buy that car.

I already kept rabbits which I bought small, then fattened and sold to the butcher. I also bought larger rabbits for breeding, and all in all made quite a bit of money from that venture. Enough anyway to start paying my school friends to help me collect old newspapers and any other junk that we might turn into a profit. Somebody knew how to fix radios, another repaired old bicycles which we then painted and sold for a fair sum.

Capitalising on the rabbit-breeding success, I decided to invest in hens. When I came back from the market carrying a crate of birds, my father was furious but in the end agreed I could keep them on condition that they were entirely my responsibility. He even agreed to let me sell the eggs to him. Luckily we had a big garden, but even so it got very crowded in there with all the hens and rabbits. When he saw that I was serious about making and saving money, I think he was actually proud of my enterprise. Ultimately I was able to sell him the old hens for the pot at a good profit!

I also used to fish on the lake in an old rowing boat I had bought. I set off by myself, sometimes as early as four-thirty in the morning, when the sun was only just appearing behind the mountains. The lake was wonderfully quiet at that time, and by breakfast I would be back at home with a bag full of fish. What we couldn't eat, I sold. >

Grilled Marinated Goat's Cheese with Potato and Apple Rösti

SERVES 4

4 × 60 g (2½ oz) goat's cheeses 30 ml (2 tablespoons) olive oil 4 sprigs each of thyme and rosemary 5 ml (1 teaspoon) lavender flowers (or extra rosemary)	Mix together and leave to marinate for at least a couple of hours.
250 g (9 oz) potatoes, peeled 1 eating apple (Granny Smith or Cox's), peeled and cored salt and freshly ground pepper	For the rösti, shred the potatoes and apple as in the next recipe, lightly season, mix well and squeeze out excess water.
45 ml (3 tablespoons) olive oil	Heat a large frying pan and wipe with a little of the olive oil. Make four rösti as in the next recipe. Keep warm. Place the goat's cheeses under a hot grill until they start bubbling and turn a light golden brown.
100–150 g (4–5 oz) mixed salad leaves, wiped and dried 15 ml (1 tablespoon) sherry vinegar	Season the leaves with salt and pepper and toss with the vinegar and the remaining olive oil. Arrange the cheeses on the rösti and surround with the dressed salad leaves.
8 walnuts, freshly shelled	Use as a garnish.

The Hotel Baeren at Twann, overlooking the lake of Bienne, where my career as a chef began in May 1962.

Apart from fishing, my other great hobby was sport. Encouraged by my father, who was himself a keen wrestler, I trained two or three times a week in the local gym. Wrestling is the Swiss national sport, and by the age of fourteen I was winning competitions and doing so well that my teachers suggested I take up sport professionally. Much as I loved the discipline and the physical feeling of well-being and personal satisfaction that came from training and keeping fit, I knew that it could never mean as much to me as food. Sport could be my hobby, but cooking had to be my living.

It was at the end of May 1962, when I was fifteen, that I

received an unexpected call from the nearby Hotel Baeren in Twann. It had about twenty bedrooms but was mainly known for the fish restaurant which overlooked a large lake. The owner of the hotel, a well-known figure, was looking for a new apprentice chef to work in the kitchens as the boy they had taken on couldn't cope with the long hours and hard work.

The hotel owner would then have been about seventy-five years old, and during his career had worked in some excellent kitchens. These included the Café Royal in London in the early 1900s, and some of the best hotels in the Middle East. In those days the hotels in cities like Cairo were wonderfully well managed, old-fashioned hotels, used to serving the best customers. So naturally I was terribly excited when he called. He had heard that I wanted to become a chef and wondered whether I would be interested in becoming an apprentice?

The very next day he drove over to our restaurant with his son-in-law, the chef, in a luxurious silver Mercedes. As he told me what my duties would be, I couldn't help staring at the starched white jacket the chef was wearing under his raincoat. I think we must have talked for an hour or more, but it was hardly necessary. I had already made up my mind that I could be ready to start in a few weeks' time.

Those weeks seemed to drag on and on, I was in such >

Berner Rösti

SERVES 4

500 g (18 oz) potatoes salt and freshly ground pepper	Peel and shred the potatoes on the rough side of a grater into a bowl, then salt lightly. Squeeze the grated potatoes with both hands to get rid of any excess moisture.
50 g (2 oz) onions, peeled and finely chopped 50 g (2 oz) lardons (little strips of bacon) 50 g (2 oz) clarified butter	Meanwhile, sweat the onions and lardons in half the butter until softened, then turn the mixture into a bowl. Add the 'dried' potatoes.
15 ml (1 tablespoon) finely chopped parsley	Add to the potato and onion mixture, stir well and season to taste. Heat a large frying pan with some of the remaining butter. Spread the potato mixture over the bottom of frying pan, and sauté well. Form into four small 'pancakes', and cook on each side until golden brown and crisp.
15 ml (1 tablespoon) finely cut chives	Sprinkle over the rösti, and serve hot.

ANTON'S TIP

A plain rösti can be made using grated potato and seasoning only. Top with a quail's egg fried in a little butter, and a teaspoon or two of caviar (type according to pocket!).

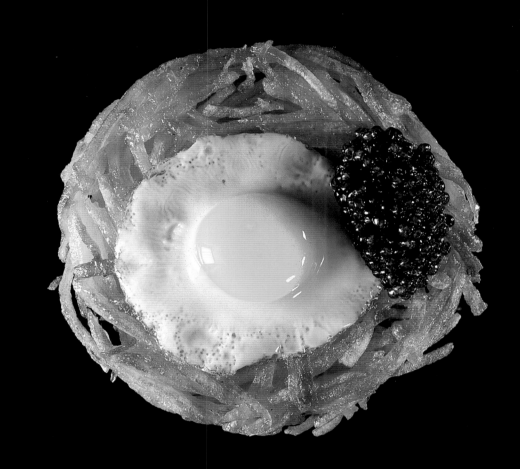

In the kitchen at the Hotel Baeren as a sixteen-year-old apprentice.

In the kitchen at the Hotel Baeren as a sixteen-year-old apprentice.

kitchen. I was set to peeling the vegetables, chopping parsley or cleaning fish, at which, of course, I had already had plenty of practice.

Monsieur Cornu, the chef, was a good teacher and an understanding chef, which was far from usual in those days. His assistant, on the other hand, was extremely temperamental, which of course was far less effective than calmly telling us what to do. Observing the differences between those two chefs taught me a lot about the way one should run a kitchen. My subsequent experience in kitchens worldwide has confirmed my belief that if you are right, it isn't necessary to shout or lose your temper, and if you are not, it won't do any good in any case.

As well as working in the kitchen, I had to attend cookery college every Wednesday to work towards my *Diplôme de Cuisine*. It was a tight schedule. I left the kitchen at twelve-fifty and only just had time for a quick wash before running all the way to the station to catch the train which left at five-past one. Still, it was one way of keeping fit.

I was never satisfied with my achievements even then, and I remember studying and reading as much as I could. Rather than going out I spent my free hour writing up my notes and preparing for the course. I found it difficult just to relax and take things easy, I was always preoccupied with wondering what and where I could do better.

I resented having to cut corners because we were always so busy, and preferred instead to get up earlier and do the job properly. Rather than give the staff packet vegetable soup for lunch, I used to get down to the kitchen in time to prepare a proper soup using fresh ingredients: potatoes as a satisfying base, with a variety of fresh greens and vegetables to add colour and substance – even nettles which I plucked from the fields behind the hotel!

Another trick I encountered then was adding 'expanders' to mayonnaise in order to make it go further. The flavour suffered. Years later, I was reminded of this when I was trying to think up an alternative to a rich egg mayonnaise, and created a much lighter and healthier version using *tofu* instead of eggs (see page 61). In Twann I also learned another 'trick of the trade' that was to prove useful throughout the years. To discourage kitchen staff from drinking the cooking wine – quite a common practice – the wine was salted!

Although the Baeren was a fish restaurant we also served a lot of game, which was always accompanied by *spätzle* (dumplings). It struck me that they would be delicious if they were flavoured with different herbs and spices, but being just a young apprentice there was no opportunity for me to try out my ideas, and indeed the

a hurry to start my job. I had told all my friends I was leaving, and now I had to sit and wait for the great day.

When it eventually came, I was half excited, half filled with apprehension. I remember my father came with me on the train to Twann, bringing my bicycle with us because although I had a small moped, I wasn't sure that I would be allowed it. I was a naturally cautious child, anxious not to create the wrong impression.

Alone in a strange place with no friends, I just had to get on as best I could. Luckily I had my own bedroom so I was able to get myself ready in private for the first day's work. I was downstairs at eight in the morning and worked through, with just an hour's break, until eleven o'clock at night.

For six days a week I was a jack-of-all-trades. Besides cooking, I shovelled snow, scrubbed floors, chopped firewood, pasted labels on to wine bottles, and carried loads so heavy that I weakened my back. It was extremely tiring work, and I could see why the other apprentice had lost heart. The one great advantage of being kept so busy, though, was that there was little time to be homesick, except at night when I got into that unfamiliar bed.

It was ten days before I could take a day's leave and return to Nidau. On the way home, I stopped off to see a few friends who, of course, wanted to hear all my stories. Thus it was quite late by the time I reached home, and my mother gave me a good scolding. But all was forgotten as we sat and talked by the fire.

In those first weeks and months as an apprentice, I was only given menial tasks, but as time went by I was gradually given more and more simple culinary jobs around the

Nettle and Potato Soup

SERVES 4

200 g (7 oz) young nettle leaves	Pick off the plants wearing gloves. Wash and drain.
15 g (½ oz) butter 15 g (½ oz) finely chopped shallots 100 g (4 oz) potatoes, peeled and finely diced	Melt the butter in a saucepan and sweat the shallot and potato for a few minutes.
800 ml (scant 1½ pints) Vegetable Stock (see page 156)	Add to the pan and simmer until the potato is very soft, about 10 minutes.
60 ml (2½ fl oz) double cream	Mix in, then add the nettle leaves. Cook for 5 minutes, then liquidise. Pass through a medium sieve, season to taste, and serve.
about 50 g (2 oz) marinated or smoked salmon, cut into shreds (optional) 4 quail's eggs, poached (optional)	Shreds of salmon and poached quail's eggs make a nice garnish.

hotel didn't expect any such input from me. Often I would wait until I was back home and try them there, but it was many years before I seriously got round to the *spätzle*. In the last few years, though, I have been able to make up for lost time and opportunity. Using the same simple, basic recipe for the dough, I've tried adding things like spinach, poppy seeds and cumin with excellent results. So it was well worth the wait (see page 24).

On one of my days off, a man came into our restaurant at home with a dozen old juke-boxes to sell. He had gone bankrupt and was prepared to do a deal on the price, so I agreed to buy the lot for 2,500 Swiss francs (about £1,000). I had no idea of their real value, I just loved the idea of being able to get them working. So I asked a school-friend to help repair the machines and put in some new records. Two weeks later I sold just one for 1,500 francs and eventually we got them all fixed and polished up and sold all, except one, which I installed at my father's restaurant. All the profits were ploughed into the car fund, of course, which was now filling up quite nicely.

It was a two and a half year apprenticeship, at the end of which it had been the custom for the last thirty-five years to send all the apprentices on to work in a hotel in Arosa, a winter holiday resort. Sometimes these former apprentices would come back to visit, and I always listened carefully to their news. Judging from their reports, the hotel didn't sound that promising, and I decided that I

would try and see if I could find somewhere better myself. I was very clear in my mind that I wanted to learn all there was to know about the business from the best teachers possible. I didn't just want to drift aimlessly from one job to the next with no specific goal. One day, I planned, I would be able to take charge of a brigade of chefs at a first-class hotel or restaurant.

So, without telling anyone, I wrote to the Palace Hotel in Villars for the post of *commis de cuisine* after my apprenticeship. To my delight I received a letter back from Hans Strässle offering me the job, on condition that I gained my *Diplôme de Cuisine*. Hans became a good friend and remains so to this day, indeed he is one of my customers!

The finals were held in a large catering college in Berne. Of the four apprentices sitting the exam that day, I was the only outsider, which naturally set me at a disadvantage since I had never used the stoves and didn't know my way around the kitchen. I was also the youngest there, and I felt extremely tense and nervous. This was, after all, one of the biggest days of my life and I really wanted to do well.

On the morning of the practical, I walked into the kitchen we were to use, and was opening my box of knives next to one of the stoves when the college head walked in. When he saw me, his face went red and he yelled in front of everyone, 'What's the matter with you? Move away. That's my stove and I'm cooking here with my girls. It's got nothing to do with you!' Considering that

I had never been in the kitchen before, it seemed a totally thoughtless and insensitive thing to do. It might well have put me off my stroke and ruined my chances in the exam. Luckily, though, I managed to keep myself together for the long day.

First came the butchery test. Then we had to fillet a fish and cut a chicken into joints before going on to cook a three-course meal. The menus were all different, drawn from a hat, so to speak, and we had to order all the ingredients we might need there and then. If one forgot something, it was bad luck. The meal I had to prepare had as a first course the Swiss Cheese and Green Onion Tart below; the second course was the classic *Filets de Sole Bonne Femme*; and the dessert was an apple baked with marzipan and raisins, with an apricot sauce. Each different meal had to be prepared at our own stoves, unaided, and in the afternoon, we had to cost it all out.

It was a difficult day, fraught with problems, though luckily there were no more for me. I felt very sorry for one poor boy whose soufflé didn't rise, which has to be one of the worst indignities to suffer in front of a group of chefs. By seven o'clock in the evening, the exams were over and we sat awaiting the results. The door opened at last and I was called up in front of the examiners and congratulated for having passed. The three others, it turned out, had failed, which meant another year's apprenticeship before they could sit the exams again. I was delighted at having passed, and later I was awarded a special diploma as the best apprentice of my year.

When I got back to Twann, Monsieur Cornu came over to offer his congratulations and a position at the hotel in Arosa. It was a difficult moment, but I had to tell him about the offer from the Palace Hotel. He was very surprised and not a little annoyed with me for having gone behind his back. He wasn't used to having his authority challenged, not least by a mere apprentice, and it was a while before he calmed down and listened to my reasons. Once he had got used to the idea, and realised that I knew what I was doing, I think he was actually rather pleased that I had taken the initiative to seek a better position. Personally I think it was one of the best decisions I have ever made.

Moving to the Palace Hotel was like leaving home all over again. This time I was much further away, too far to be able to go home on my days off. Still, my contract was just for the winter season. I was the youngest in a brigade of thirty chefs at the Palace, working under Monsieur Dessibourg.

Henri Dessibourg came from the Valais, the French-speaking part of Switzerland, and he was the picture of the traditional chef. He was in his mid-fifties and beneath

Swiss Cheese and Green Onion Tart

MAKES 1 × 20 CM (8 IN) TART   OVEN: Moderately hot, 200°C/400°F/Gas 6

225 g (8 oz) plain flour salt and freshly ground pepper 100 g (4 oz) butter, cut into small pieces 1 egg yolk 10 ml (1 dessertspoon) water	To make the pastry, sieve the flour into a bowl, season, then rub in the butter pieces until the texture resembles breadcrumbs. Bind with the egg yolk and water, and rest for about 30 minutes in the fridge. Roll out and use to line a flan ring placed on a baking sheet. Cover with foil, fill with baking beans, and bake blind in the preheated oven for 10 minutes. Remove and cool. Reduce the temperature of the oven to 180°C/350°F/Gas 4.
50 g (2 oz) butter 4 oz (100 g) spring onions (about 2 bunches), coarsely cut	For the filling, melt the butter, and sweat the spring onions over a low heat until soft but not pulpy.
75 g (3 oz) Emmenthal cheese, grated 50 g (2 oz) Gruyère cheese, grated	Sprinkle into the par-baked pastry case, then add the spring onions.
2 eggs 100 ml (3½ fl oz) each of single cream and milk freshly grated nutmeg	Mix together, adding salt, pepper and nutmeg to taste. Pour into the pastry case, and bake in the oven for 20–25 minutes until lightly set. Serve warm.

SAISON D'HIVER
1964-65
VILLARS PALACE

the taut white cotton of his chef's jacket, lay a stomach truly worthy of its owner's status. Naturally he spoke only French, in a loud booming voice. But though his voice was loud, his heart was good, unlike that of his German-speaking assistant, who used to be called upon to translate the chef's instructions from French to German. He used to waddle up to me and shout out the commands, his face inflamed with the exertion. He got the job done, but only by terrorising us and risking his health. Discipline had to be learned, I could see, but surely not by yelling at people?

Monsieur Dessibourg ran an extremely efficient kitchen, and no detail escaped his attention. Each vegetable, although there were eight individual chefs cutting them, had to be cut to the same size, and every single blemish removed. Yet only 10 per cent wastage was tolerated. (Often these exact dice would then be puréed for a *gazpacho!*) Whatever you were doing, you had to constantly produce your best work or the chef would tell you off, and he was capable of reducing even grown men to tears. But those who followed his instruction to the letter were rewarded and recognised for their work. It may have been a tough, old-fashioned regime, but I was impressed.

After the Baeren, where I had been given anything and everything to do, my days at the Palace seemed more like a holiday. Instead of rushing frantically from one job to the next, I was now a *commis entremétier*, and could concentrate all my efforts on making sure that I prepared the vegetables, soups, pasta etc. to perfection.

Working with the eight others in my section, I happily peeled, sliced and chopped from eight-thirty or nine o'clock each morning. At ten-thirty we stopped for lunch, which was always half an hour. There was no question of taking an extra few minutes as Monsieur Dessibourg sat at the head of our table, and at exactly half a minute to eleven he would be watching the time, ready to jump up at eleven on the dot.

He was so determined that we should be back at our work stations punctually that he wouldn't let us see the post even though the letters used to arrive during lunch. We always had to wait until the afternoon break. Sometimes I could see in amongst the pile a pink envelope which I knew was from my girlfriend. My patience would be sorely tried during those two and a half hours, longing for them to pass so that I could tear open the envelope and read what was inside.

When I was in Los Angeles recently, I heard another amusing story about Henri Dessibourg, from Kurt Fischer. (He had been *chef garde-manger* at the Palace at that time, and is now the vice-president of Westin International, a large hotel chain.) Apparently every morning at ten the housekeeper would phone down to the kitchen for the chef, and he would disappear. One day, he wasn't there when the call came through, and the message left was: *'Le bain est prêt'* (the bath is ready). Thus it was discovered that Monsieur Dessibourg had a bath drawn and readied for him by the hotel housekeeper at that time

Monsieur Dessibourg surrounded by his kitchen brigade, myself third from the left in the second back row. The pastry chef fourth from the left in the top row was always so hungry that he would walk out of the kitchen with a foil-wrapped, freshly roasted chicken under his hat for a midnight feast.

every day, and that the pot-washer – an employee of very long standing – would daily wash his hair! I do seem to remember how immaculate the chef would look at our early lunch, nicely shaved, with his fair, freshly curled hair.

The hotel had quite a few retired guests who would come to stay for the whole winter, bringing with them their dogs, who also had to be fed. Two chefs were given the job each day of preparing the dogs' dinners. There was no question of simply serving up leftovers under Henri Dessibourg. He insisted they should have freshly cooked meals and this peculiar responsibility fell to one *chef*

entremétier since he looked after the *à la carte* dishes.

'*Un steak de veau, grillé sans sel, pour un chien!*' came the order. I should think we must have spent a good half hour each evening, carefully turning carrots and preparing a decent cut of meat just for a dog. Sometimes it got too much for the poor *chef entremétier*.

'*Ah! encore ces chiens emmerdants!*' he'd curse.

It seems incredible, but for Monsieur Dessibourg the dogs were almost as important as the guests. He was so precise, so disciplined and so exact that even their food had to be perfect.

Herb Spätzle

SERVES 4

50 g (2 oz) fresh young spinach	Wash the leaves, and place still wet in the food processor. Add 15–45 ml (1–3 tablespoons) water and whizz to mash well, but not purée.
50 g (2 oz) mixed green herbs (flat-leaf parsley, basil, sage)	Wash, dry, add to the food processor, and whizz briefly.
4 eggs 250 g (9 oz) plain flour salt freshly grated nutmeg	Place in a bowl and beat together with a wooden spoon. Add the spinach and herb purée.
milk	Add enough milk – up to 25 ml (1 fl oz) – to make a soft dough. Beat well against the sides of the bowl with a wooden spoon until air bubbles to the surface of the dough. Leave to rest for 30 minutes in the fridge.
15 ml (1 tablespoon) sunflower oil	Add to a large pan of boiling salted water. Spread the herb dough over the surface of a small chopping board, then, using a palette knife, drop small lines of the dough over the edge into the boiling water. When the *spätzle* rise to the top of the water, remove with a slotted spoon and put into cold water. Remove and drain well when cold.
25–50 g (1–2 oz) butter 2 shallots, peeled and finely chopped 1 small red pepper, seeded and cut into strips	Sweat together in a pan until the vegetables have softened a little. Add the *spätzle* and heat through gently.
shavings of fresh Parmesan cheese	Serve hot with shavings of Parmesan over each serving.

ANTON'S TIP

These light 'dumplings', a speciality in many eastern European countries, can be simmered in soups, mixed with vegetables, topped with stews or served by themselves. They make a good accompaniment for dishes with sauces, especially game.

There are various types of *spätzle* makers on the market, ranging from a grater with large perforations to ricer and food-mill type implements. You could improvise with a colander through which you can push the dough.

Chapter Two

An Italian Summer

LOOKING UP FROM MY CHOPPING BOARD, I COULD SEE THE HOTEL FORECOURT THROUGH THE KITCHEN WINDOW, AND AS I WORKED, I WOULD OFTEN NOTICE YOUNG MEN DRIVE UP IN THEIR OPEN-TOP SPORTS CARS, GIRLFRIENDS BY THEIR SIDES. THIS FILLED ME WITH LONGING, AND FUELLED A DETERMINATION TO WORK EVEN HARDER.

IT WAS AFTER MY EIGHTEENTH BIRTHDAY THAT I FINALLY SAVED ENOUGH MONEY TO BE ABLE TO BUY A CAR. NOT THE CORVAIR, FOR IT NOW SEEMED TOO BIG AND SHOWY, AND IN ANY CASE WAS STILL WAY BEYOND MY MEANS. BUT I COULD AFFORD A TRIUMPH SPIT-FIRE. IT WAS A BEAUTY, WHITE OUTSIDE WITH RED LEATHER UPHOLSTERY, AND I LOVED IT PASSIONATELY (THE BEGINNING OF A LIFE-LONG PASSION). WITH A LITTLE FINANCIAL HELP FROM MY MOTHER I WAS ABLE TO START HAVING DRIVING LESSONS AND BY THE SUMMER I COULD DRIVE AND WAS RARING TO GO.

I WANTED TO WORK ABROAD, AND WITH THE HELP OF HENRI DESSIBOURG, I WAS OFFERED A JOB AS *COMMIS GARDE-MANGER*, HELPING TO PREPARE THE SALADS, COLD SOUPS AND COLD *ENTREES*, FOR THE SUMMER SEASON AT THE CAVALIERI HILTON IN ROME. I WAS SO EXCITED AND THRILLED THAT I KEPT THE TELEGRAM AND ENVELOPE WHICH CAME TO ME FROM ITALY — I HAVE THEM STILL!

THIS TIME I WASN'T SETTING OFF ON MY OWN TO A STRANGE HOTEL, I WAS GOING WITH three other friends from the Palace Hotel which was some relief since it was the first time I had left Switzerland to work. And, although I had picked up a smattering of Italian phrases from various Italian chefs, it wasn't much to go on.

I loved that drive to Rome in my first car. I suppose it must have been about six on Sunday evening when I reached the city, and I soon got myself completely lost trying to find the hotel. In the end I asked another driver, but his directions were so complicated he offered to show me the way. Before I had time to think he was off and I had to put my foot down to catch up. We raced through the narrow streets, him gaily hooting at dogs, cats and anything that got in the way, whilst I just did my best to keep up. It was a hair-raising, completely mad dash, but it certainly got me quickly acclimatised to Roman driving. We soon found the Hilton, and I was able at last to join my friends, my heart racing and thankful to be in one piece!

The chef, René Rastello, also came from the Valais, and was well-known within the Hilton group. He was another of the loud, aggressive school of chefs, and once thumped the table so hard that he broke his finger. Not

only was he very strict about discipline and good organisation, but he kept an iron-handed grip on the budget. From him I was to learn a good deal about the importance of accurate costing, and how crucial it was to the success of any enterprise, but I also became aware of some of the dangers. I was convinced that the chef ended up losing more than he gained by cutting costs with the staff's food budget. Whenever the staff chef made a purchasing order, the list would be returned with at least half of the items crossed out in red ink. These weren't extravagances, but basics like oil and butter, and since the staff clearly had to be fed somehow, the desperate staff chef often took matters into his own hands.

The other chefs were well aware of what was going on, so they took care never to leave anything out on the tables. But that didn't stop the staff chef wandering around the kitchen, stopping for a chat and then, whilst you weren't looking, pinching something from you. I remember once, when making some mayonnaise, I innocently left two bottles of oil besides the mixing bowl while going to the larder to get some salt. When I got back a few seconds later the

My beloved first car, a Triumph Spitfire, for which I had saved up since I was twelve years old, and in which I made that momentous trip to Rome.

bottles had disappeared and nobody would own up. The oil had simply vanished, so I had to go and explain – with some considerable difficulty – why I needed some more.

That problem just snowballed, and the kitchen staff felt so hard done-by that they considered it justifiable to take almost anything they needed. Standing in the lunch queue one day, I discovered where some of the missing items went. In front of me stood a couple of chambermaids. The first girl was happy, but the second said she didn't like *spaghetti bolognese*, the dish of the day. Couldn't she have her *spaghetti 'al burro'*? The staff cook smiled indulgently, and then brought out from beneath the counter some 'borrowed' butter and some fresh basil which he carefully arranged on her plate.

It was a lively, busy kitchen and before long I had soon picked up a good deal of Italian and had made plenty of new friends. One was a butcher called Migueli who was veritably Italian, with hair coloured black and a moustache which he considered the most important feature of his appearance. Each day he would spend at least ten minutes in front of the mirror to persuade it into the correct shape. Five years later, on the other side of the world (in Montreal), I was to meet him again, and his moustache was still his major vanity, demanding a lot of time and attention in front of a mirror.

Another friend, one of the more colourful chefs, was also a Migueli. He came from Ischia, and salads and *hors d'oeuvres* were his great speciality. During the six months I worked with him, we must have made at least twenty different salads every day, and yet we never repeated any combinations during that time.

He was extremely clever and had an instinctive understanding of how to combine flavours and textures to create something exciting and delicious. I remember when I first tasted his version of *gazpacho*. It was wonderful, pungent and alive with the taste of the ripest tomatoes and the freshest oregano. It was undoubtedly the best *gazpacho* I had ever tasted, and today it is still Migueli's recipe that I use. But of all the things I remember about that remarkable man, it was the way he tasted the soup. He would take a good drink from the ladle, and then tip the rest back in the pot leaving the ends of his moustache dripping!

Though he was a good friend of mine, Migueli never really got on with another Swiss called Gebi, who was an inveterate tease. One afternoon when I returned to the kitchen at about five o'clock after my break, neither of them were to be seen. I couldn't think what had happened to Gebi as he was never late, but thought no more about it and started to get on with my work. It must have >

Gazpacho

SERVES 4

200 g (7 oz) good tomatoes, skinned and coarsely chopped 100 g (4 oz) cucumber, peeled and diced 30 g (1¼ oz) finely chopped onion 30 g (1¼ oz) coarsely chopped red and green peppers ½ garlic clove, peeled and very finely chopped 15 g (½ oz) fresh white breadcrumbs	Mix together in a large bowl or pan.
20 ml (4 teaspoons) red wine vinegar 50 ml (2 fl oz) White Poultry Stock (see page 156) 40 ml (1½ fl oz) olive oil a few fresh oregano leaves 3 basil leaves salt and freshly ground pepper	Add, and season with salt and pepper. Leave to marinate for 12 hours in the fridge. Liquidise to make a fine purée then strain through a sieve.
50 ml (2 fl oz) single cream	Add, stir in, and taste again for seasoning. Chill.
3 basil leaves, cut in fine strips	Use as a garnish. Serve cold, possibly on ice.

Zucchini and Saffron Risotto

SERVES 4

25 g (1 oz) butter	Melt in a suitable pan.
1 small onion, peeled and finely chopped	Add, and cook gently without colouring for about 2–3 minutes.
200 g (7 oz) arborio rice	Add, stirring to coat the rice thoroughly with butter, using a spatula. Do not let anything brown.
a good pinch of saffron threads approx. 1 litre (1¾ pints) hot White Poultry Stock or Vegetable Stock (see page 156), well seasoned	Add the saffron and about 150 ml (5 fl oz) of the hot stock to begin with, and start stirring. The rice will immediately begin to get creamy (as the starch is released). Over a medium heat keep adding simmering stock in similar small quantities to retain that creamy consistency as the rice absorbs the stock.
250 g (9 oz) small courgettes, trimmed and blanched	Halve lengthwise, scrape out the middles, and slice thinly into crescents. Add when the rice is a few minutes from ready (soft outside but with an inner firmness).
50 ml (2 fl oz) dry white wine	Add just a few seconds before you judge the rice to be finally ready. This stops the cooking. Remove from the heat.
butter (optional) freshly grated Parmesan cheese salt and freshly ground pepper 30 ml (2 tablespoons) finely cut chives	Stir in a knob of butter if you like, with some Parmesan to taste, and taste for seasoning (the stock should have flavoured the rice, and the cheese if fairly salty). Sprinkle with chives and serve immediately, with a separate bowl of grated Parmesan from which guests can help themselves.

been a few minutes before I went over to the walk-in fridge to get some eggs. I opened the heavy door, and found Migueli inside, holding a big knife to Gebi's throat.

'*Una parola di più . . .*' (one more word), he threatened, his face puce.

I tried to calm him down. 'You know what Gebi's like, forget it, Migueli. He doesn't mean it . . .'

Eventually Migueli loosened his grip and let Gebi go, but not without a good deal more knife-waving and cursing as he went back to his station.

But hot tempers soon blow over in the kitchen and we had a busy evening ahead preparing for a large cold buffet. A constant star of the Cavalieri buffet was one particular and unfortunate turkey which reappeared throughout the season in a number of different guises. Of the original bird all that remained was the carcass and legs, no breast. When we wanted to use it, we filled the breast >

FROM THE BEGINNING, EAC

AND IN ORDER TO SUCCEEI

I WANTED TO WORK ONLY '

DROP IN SALARY OR STATU!

I WAS AWARE THAT, IN THE

 OF MY CAREER WAS PLANNED WITH ONE GOAL IN MIND,

 D NOT WASTE TIME WORKING IN A BADLY ORGANISED KITCHEN.

 FELT I COULD LEARN, AND SO I PREFERRED TO TAKE A TEMPORARY

 DER TO WORK UNDER A GOOD CHEF OR IN A NEW POSITION BECAUSE

 UN, THE EXPERIENCE WOULD PAY DIVIDENDS.

cavity with rice cooked in milk to which gelatine had been added. This gave it form. The breast was then reshaped and fresh slices of turkey were arranged on top and decorated with glazing and various garnishes. When it was finished, it looked very impressive. Of course as soon as the buffet was over, the denuded bird was carried back to the kitchen without the meat and put back in the freezer! Hardly *Cuisine Naturelle*, but nevertheless ingenious.

Rice is a wonderfully versatile food and that particular usage of it was only one of many that I learned in Rome. My favourite way of cooking it, then and now, is to make a simple *risotto* flavoured with saffron, courgettes or wild mushrooms. Only last autumn I went mushroom-picking with the kitchen brigade in a wood in Kent, cooked and ate some there, and returned with enough *porcini, chanterelles* and horn of plenty to serve a lunch party of five visiting Italian businessmen with *risotto*.

Although René Rastello kept a tight rein on the finances, he was generous with our time off. We worked split-duty every day, and had two or three hours off in the afternoon which we often spent going to the seaside. Rome, of course, was a wonderful place to spend the summer and most nights after work, we would all gather in our favourite cafés. I ate out a lot then, exploring all the new tastes and combinations. In one trattoria, I tasted some wonderful fish starters, which I always followed with >

Marinated Sweet and Sour Pink Trout

SERVES 4

4 pink rainbow trout, filleted and skinned	Remove all the bones, using tweezers. Place the fillets flat in one layer in a dish with sides.
salt and freshly ground pepper about 10 ml (2 teaspoons) caster sugar	Season the fillets.
25 g (1 oz) pine kernels 4 shallots or small red onions, peeled and finely sliced into rings 25 g (1 oz) sultanas 15 ml (1 tablespoon) capers, drained	Sprinkle over the fillets.
2 small carrots, peeled	Score with a cannelle knife, then slice finely and blanch quickly. Add to the trout dish.
approx. 200 ml (7 fl oz) white wine vinegar	Pour over, and leave to marinate for at least 12 hours in a cool place. Remove the fillets from the marinade and arrange on a platter or individual plates.
a few sprigs of fresh fennel, dill or chervil a handful of fresh green leaves (young spinach, rocket or lamb's lettuce) a few rings of red pepper	Use to garnish the trout fillets, along with some of the marinade ingredients and a little of the liquid.

Baked Marinated Sardines

SERVES 4   OVEN: Moderately hot, 200°C/400°F/Gas 6

12 fresh medium sardines salt and freshly ground pepper	Scale, remove the heads and guts, and trim the fins and tails. Clean and pat dry, then season.
50 ml (2 fl oz) olive oil	Brush a little over a shallow ovenproof dish, and arrange the sardines in it. Place in the preheated oven and bake for a few minutes while you prepare the mixture. 　　Meanwhile, gently heat a frying pan with the rest of the olive oil.
4 shallots, peeled and finely sliced 1 garlic clove, peeled and crushed 2.5 ml (½ tsp) fennel seeds, crushed	Add to the oil in the pan, and sweat until the mixture is soft, about 5 minutes.
200 g (7 oz) tomatoes, skinned, seeded and roughly chopped 60 g (2¼ oz) oil-cured black olives, pitted 60 ml (4 tablespoons) white wine 30 g (1¼ oz) capers	Add to the pan, and bring to the boil. Pour over the sardines in the dish, and continue cooking in the oven until the sardines are golden in colour, about 4–6 minutes.
30 ml (2 tablespoons) freshly chopped parsley 5 ml (1 teaspoon) freshly chopped oregano	Sprinkle over the fish and serve.

IT HAS ALWAYS BEEN MY PHILOSOPHY THAT A CHEF SHOULD BE CONSTANTLY

IN TOUCH WITH HIS GROWERS AND SUPPLIERS. AS I WOULD

NEVER BRING ANYTHING WITH ME TO A NEW COUNTRY EXCEPT

INSIST ON BUYING MY INGREDIENTS FROM THE LOCAL SHOPS.

Ravioli with Cottage Cheese, Watercress and Pine Kernels

SERVES 4

1 quantity Home-Made Egg Noodle dough (any colour, see next page)	Make, wrap in foil or a damp cloth, and allow to rest for at least 2 hours.
15 ml (1 tablespoon) olive oil 50 g (2 oz) shallots, peeled and finely chopped ½ garlic clove, peeled and very finely chopped	For the filling, sweat together in a frying pan for 2 minutes. Remove from the heat and transfer the mixture to a bowl to cool.
15 ml (1 tablespoon) roughly cut fresh coriander 100 g (4 oz) cottage cheese, drained 15 ml (1 tablespoon) pine kernels, toasted 1 bunch watercress, leaves only, finely cut 30 g (1¼ oz) fresh brown or white breadcrumbs salt and freshly ground pepper	Stir into the onion mixture, and season with salt and pepper. Unwrap the noodle dough, divide in two, and roll each piece out thinly to similar sizes. Place one piece on a flat surface. Place teaspoons of the filling at even intervals over the sheet of pasta. Using water and a brush, moisten the lines between the filling mounds, then cover with the second rolled-out piece of dough. Using your fingertips, carefully press down the top sheet around the mounds of filling to make 'parcels'. Using a pastry cutter or a sharp knife, cut the ravioli into individual sealed squares. Press the edges again to secure. Reserve on a baking sheet dusted with flour. Cook ravioli in plenty of boiling salted water for 2–3 minutes until *al dente*. Drain well.
30 ml (2 tablespoons) olive oil 60 ml (4 tablespoons) tomato *concassée*, warmed through	Toss the ravioli with the oil, and sprinkle with the warmed tomato *concassée*.
15 ml (1 tablespoon) finely cut fresh coriander 50 g (2 oz) Parmesan cheese, freshly grated	Serve immediately, sprinkled with the coriander and Parmesan.

ANTON'S TIP

To make tomato *concassée*, make a light cut in the skin of each tomato, immerse in boiling water for 10 seconds, and then remove. Peel off the skin, and halve the tomato. Spoon out the seeds, then chop the flesh very finely.

To make a tomato paste or purée, simply blend tomato *concassée* in a liquidiser or blender.

IVES, SO I ALWAYS

spaghetti carbonara. One of them was a sweet and sour fish, which was unfamiliar to me but very delicious. The other was a baked sardine dish which utilised ingredients which characterised Italy for me – olives, olive oil from the local olive groves, capers, oregano, tomatoes and fennel seeds.

On Sundays I was often invited back to the Italian chefs' homes. We would set off individually in our cars, and would arrive in their home villages by midday. Usually Mama, grandmother or one of the aunts would have spent the morning making the pasta and the sauce. Of course each one had their own, unique recipe of which they were fiercely proud. One would have pounded a *pesto* with fresh basil and pine kernels, another made a tomato sauce, and sometimes we just had plain olive oil and a few leaves of basil. To this day when I smell fresh basil, it brings back the memories of that time. >

I'm an avid collector – of cars, books, menus, recipes and mementoes such as this telegram. I still keep everything.

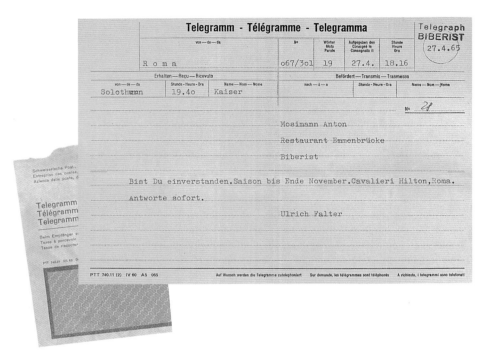

It was wonderful to be able to watch them make the pasta and to see how they swiftly and deftly rolled and sliced the floury strips of dough with such confidence. I learned so much from those ladies, and today pasta – home-made and in many varieties – is still a great favourite, both to make and eat.

Ravioli filled with meat or Ricotta and spinach was another pasta dish I loved, and over the years I have tried all kinds of alternative fillings. Feta cheese with spinach makes a delicious combination, but cottage cheese, I discovered, made an excellent light and low-cholesterol variation. But of course you could use tomato *concassée*, a purée of vegetables or really anything you fancy. I would then design a sauce to complement the filling. The secret, I think, is always to keep it simple, and to use your common sense and creativity.

Those days come back to me so clearly now as I see us sitting round the scrubbed wooden tables, with bottles of good home-made wine. The food was simple, but prepared from the heart, with love, and from the best of >

Home-Made Egg Noodles

SERVES 4

200 g (7 oz) strong plain white flour (or fine wholewheat flour), sieved 25 g (1 oz) semolina	Mix together in a bowl and make a well in the centre.
1 egg, beaten 15 ml (1 tablespoon) olive oil a good pinch of salt 45–60 ml (3–4 tablespoons) hot water	Place in the well in the flour, and gradually work the flour in towards the middle. Knead into a very firm, smooth dough. Wrap in a damp cloth, and allow to rest in a cool place for at least 2–3 hours. Divide into five pieces and roll each piece as thinly as possible. Lay the pieces on top of each other and cut into strips approximately 6 mm (¼ in) wide. Cook while fresh, or leave to dry. Boil fresh noodles for 2–3 minutes in salted water, or about double that time if dried.

Black Ink Noodles
Make exactly as above, but add at least 40 ml (1½ fl oz) of squid ink to the dough instead of the water.

Saffron Noodles
Make exactly as above, but dissolve a large pinch of saffron threads in the hot water first before proceeding.

Spinach Noodles
Make exactly as above but add 50 g (2 oz) purée of spinach instead of the hot water, adding a little warm water if necessary.

Tomato Noodles
Make exactly as above, but add 15 ml (1 tablespoon) tomato purée instead of the hot water.

Piccata of Veal Cavalieri

SERVES 4

Ingredients	Method
12 × 30 g (1¼ oz) thin slices of veal fillet, beaten to flatten salt and freshly ground white pepper a little flour for dusting	Season the pieces of veal and dust with flour.
2 eggs, beaten 20 g (¾ oz) Parmesan cheese, freshly grated	Mix together and use to coat the veal pieces.
40 ml (1½ fl oz) olive oil 40 g (1½ oz) butter	Heat together in a pan, then sauté the veal pieces in it, gently moving the pan, until golden brown. Keep warm.
200 g (7 oz) ripe tomatoes, skinned, seeded and diced	Drain off most of their juices, then sauté in the oil and butter remaining in the pan. Arrange on top of the veal pieces, and season.
80 g (3¼ oz) Mozzarella cheese, sliced 20 ml (¾ fl oz) double cream 15 ml (1 tablespoon) chopped fresh oregano	Lay the Mozzarella on top of the tomato and brush with the cream. Sprinkle with oregano, and melt the cheese under a hot grill.
300 g (10 oz) fresh Spinach Noodles (see page 36) 30 g (1¼ oz) butter	Meanwhile, cook the noodles in boiling salted water until *al dente*, then drain well. Mix in the butter, and arrange on warmed serving plates. Place the carefully seasoned meat on top.
200 ml (7 fl oz) Marsala Sauce (see Tip)	Serve in a sauce boat to accompany the veal and noodles.

ingredients – vegetables, fruit and the wonderful Italian cheeses. A basic ingredient such as potato could be made into gnocchi and transformed by the strong tang of blue cheese and fresh herbs used in a sauce.

After we had eaten, we would explore the village and the countryside, and I learned more about my colleagues and Italians in general. They were so welcoming, and their homes and families so friendly and easy-going. It was quite different from the intense pressure and tense atmosphere that reigned in the hotel kitchens.

I've never forgotten one of those meals eaten in Italy, and even today I never forget whether a meal was good, bad or indifferent. The good ones always inspire other ideas, the bad ones remind me of the pitfalls, and the indifferent are so depressing it only strengthens my resolve never to be like that. When someone serves hard melon or undercooked pheasant I'm annoyed because they could both so easily have been avoided.

All too soon the summer season ended. I had enjoyed my stay in Italy very much and had learned a lot at the Cavalieri – and from the families of my fellow chefs. Some of the most popular dishes on the hotel menu I still cook today, although I always adapt the basic ideas. The veal in Italy, for instance, was of superb quality, and I loved *Osso Buco*, the classic Italian shin of veal dish. I also cook *piccata*, small slices of veal, and serve them with a Marsala sauce. I named the latter recipe after the hotel in salute.

From Italy I returned to Switzerland for a business course in Lucerne. When the winter season began I went to the Waldhaus in Sils-Maria, high in the Swiss Alps, where there was a small friendly kitchen of just fifteen chefs. Here I worked as *commis saucier* under Monsieur Näf. One of the main things I remember about the Waldhaus, apart from the joy of being in the mountains again, was the old coal-fired stove. As a junior chef I had to keep a good fire going. By the afternoon, my head used to ache terribly and it took a while until I realised that it was due to the amount of coal dust I inhaled. >

Spinach Gnocchi with Stilton

SERVES 4

600 g (1 lb, 5 oz) potatoes, washed	Cook in their skins, peel whilst hot, then push through a fine sieve into a bowl.
150 g (5 oz) plain flour 2 eggs, beaten	Blend in carefully, and stir well until smooth.
15 ml (1 tablespoon) finely cut lemon thyme 100 g (4 oz) spinach purée, dried well salt and freshly ground pepper freshly grated nutmeg	Mix in the herb, then add enough of the spinach purée to achieve a good colour. Season to taste with salt, pepper and nutmeg. Pipe or roll the mixture into a long log of approximately 2.5 cm (1 in) in diameter and cut into 3.5 cm (1½ in) lengths. Dust well with extra flour and roll each piece in your hands. Press with the tip of a fork to make a pattern. Poach in boiling salted water for about 5 minutes and then drain carefully.
100 ml (3½ fl oz) each of *fromage frais* and double cream 150 g (5 oz) Stilton (or Gorgonzola) cheese, crumbled	For the sauce, reduce the creams together in a pan, then add the crumbled cheese, stirring over a low heat until melted. Reheat the gnocchi gently in the sauce for about 2 minutes.
30 ml (2 tablespoons) mixed finely cut herbs (chives, basil, lemon thyme)	Add to the sauce, season to taste again, and serve hot.

A postcard of the Waldhaus Hotel, Sils-Maria, in 1965, where I spent the winter season after I left Rome.

After leaving the Waldhaus I took another diploma, this time in diet and health, at the hotel school in Lucerne. Even then I felt that there must be a healthier way of preparing food than just producing the heavy, cream- and fat-laden classic dishes with which we were familiar. It was an interesting course that took us through a range of different kinds of diet. The most difficult was when we had to prepare a meal without salt. We substituted an assortment of herbs for flavour, again something I later developed in creating *Cuisine Naturelle*.

I then studied for a diploma in carving, table serving and *flambé* work, but when the season ended I still wanted to learn more so I enrolled on a two-year correspondence course in book-keeping, communication and the business side of the trade, leading to a diploma in commerce. I wanted to be quite sure that I gave myself as varied and solid a grounding in my chosen career as it was possible to acquire. That way I hoped to avoid mistakes later on. But first there was more travelling to do.

Osso Buco

SERVES 4   OVEN: Moderate, 180°C/350°F/Gas 4

4 × 250 g (9 oz) *osso buco* pieces (shin of veal) salt and freshly ground pepper flour for dusting	Season the *osso buco* pieces and lightly dust with flour.
30 ml (2 tablespoons) groundnut oil	Heat in a large casserole – one big enough to take the veal pieces in one layer – and brown the meat on each side. Take care not to lose the marrow from the bones. Remove meat from the casserole and keep warm.
50 g (2 oz) onion, peeled and finely chopped 1 garlic clove, peeled and crushed 150 g (5 oz) in total of trimmed carrot, celeriac, celery and leek, cut into small dice 5 ml (1 teaspoon) chopped fresh thyme and basil	Sauté in the oil remaining in the casserole for a few minutes.
20 g (¾ oz) tomato purée (see Tip on page 35) 75 g (3 oz) tomatoes, skinned, seeded and chopped 150 ml (5 fl oz) white wine	Add and cook gently until reduced by a third.
1.5 litres (2½ pints) White Veal Stock (see page 156)	Add half of the stock, along with the meat, to the casserole, bring to the boil on top of the stove, cover then cook in the preheated oven until the veal is tender, about 2 hours. If necessary, add more of the veal stock.
5 ml (1 teaspoon) grated lemon rind ½ garlic clove, peeled and chopped 15 ml (1 tablespoon) chopped parsley	Mix together and sprinkle this *gremolata* over the *osso buco*. Serve from the casserole.

Chapter Three

The Canadian Experience

AFTER ALL THIS HARD WORK, I FELT READY TO TRAVEL AGAIN AND WHEN I HEARD THAT CHEFS WERE BEING SOUGHT FOR EXPO '67 IN MONTREAL, I DIDN'T NEED TO THINK TWICE. WORKING IN A COMPLETELY UNKNOWN COUNTRY WAS TOO GOOD AN OPPORTUNITY TO MISS. TO GET THE FEEL OF IT, I WENT OUT TO MONTREAL ALMOST A YEAR IN ADVANCE OF EXPO, IN JUNE 1966, AND TOOK ON THE POSITION OF *CHEF TOURNANT* AT THE QUEEN ELIZABETH HOTEL IN MONTREAL. THIS WAS *THE* HOTEL WITHIN THE HILTON GROUP, IN SIZE, MANAGEMENT AND IN ITS REPUTATION FOR TEACHING. THE KITCHEN WAS RUN BY A CELEBRATED SWISS CHEF, ALBERT SCHNELL. ALTHOUGH THE POSITION WAS SUPPOSED TO BE ONLY SHORT-TERM, THINGS TURNED OUT VERY DIFFERENTLY.

BEFORE LEAVING FOR CANADA, I WENT HOME TO SEE MY PARENTS. I HAD, HOWEVER, ONLY BEEN THERE A SHORT WHILE WHEN MY MOTHER BECAME ILL. SHE DIED SOON AFTER, AND IN THE CIRCUMSTANCES I WANTED TO POSTPONE THE TRIP. BUT MY FATHER WAS ADAMANT THAT IT WOULD BE THE BEST THING FOR ME TO DO, AND THAT MY MOTHER WOULD HAVE WISHED IT. THERE WAS, HE INSISTED, NOTHING MORE I COULD DO AT HOME. SO IT WAS WITH A HEAVY HEART THAT I BOARDED THE AEROPLANE TO MONTREAL.

I WAS JUST NINETEEN YEARS OLD AND ALONE IN A STRANGE COUNTRY WHERE I KNEW

The Queen Elizabeth Hotel in Montreal, Canada, where I worked with the celebrated Swiss chef, Albert Schnell, during Expo '67.

no-one. My feeling of loneliness was compounded on my arrival at the Queen Elizabeth Hotel, a daunting grey concrete building with 1,200 rooms and over 2,000 staff. Built eight years before, it seemed at first sight to have no atmosphere or warmth. In the kitchen, however, things were different. With eleven restaurants to run and 150 chefs in the brigade, Albert Schnell performed a remarkable task, and once I had settled in to the rhythms of his kitchen, I began to feel more at home.

Albert was a great teacher and organiser, capable, in spite of the large numbers, of motivating his chefs to produce the highest quality work. This was a man, I sensed immediately, from whom I would learn much. He employed chefs from all over the world and in all I think there must have been about fifteen different nationalities under one roof. There were Canadians, Japanese and many Europeans, though I think there were probably more French and Greeks than anything else, and yet we all worked quite happily side by side, learning just enough of one another's languages to get by.

By the time Expo opened, I was working full stretch. I did the morning shift at the Canadian Pavilion, as *sous chef*, and returned to the Queen Elizabeth in the afternoon and evening. In other words, I worked from seven in the morning through to nearly midnight, day in day out, for about three months with no days off. Quite often I would be half asleep on my way into work the next morning, but somehow I managed to get through each day. I think I survived mainly on exhilaration and the thought that when I eventually returned to my apartment I could enjoy the sauna and swimming pool that came with it.

There were endless official visits to the Pavilion and hundreds of guest for lunch or dinner at the hotel, so the brigades in both kitchens were working under constant pressure. The knowledge that we were cooking for some of the most successful and celebrated people in the world helped! Some 95 per cent of the world's presidents were staying at the Queen Elizabeth and had to be catered for at dinner whilst a constant stream of celebrities visited the Pavilion. One of the most successful dishes we prepared there was lobster soufflé. The meat was served inside the shell with a soufflé mixture on top. It was a wonderful recipe, but perhaps a little too rich for today's taste. Another new dish for me was a lobster cocktail which I still prepare today, except that now I cook the lobster very lightly, which keeps the flesh tender, and instead of the traditional American cocktail sauce, I serve it with a lighter one of my own, based on yoghurt, orange and lemon juices and fresh dill. >

Lobster Cocktail

SERVES 4

2 × 450 g (1 lb) lobsters, freshly cooked	Cut the flesh into pieces while still warm.
50 g (2 oz) mustard and cress	Divide between four suitable glasses or glass dishes.
200 g (7 oz) natural yoghurt 50 ml (2 fl oz) each of fresh orange and lemon juices 15 ml (1 tablespoon) finely snipped dill salt and freshly ground pepper 5 ml (1 teaspoon) brandy (optional)	Mix together to make a sauce. Divide between the four glasses or dishes, and place the lobster flesh on top.
4 lemon wedges	Use as a garnish, and serve while the lobster is still lukewarm.

ANTON'S TIP

You could add further garnishing ingredients if you liked – sliced hard-boiled egg, for instance – but to me this is a very simple and honest recipe as it is.

The seafood available in Montreal was a revelation to someone coming from a land-locked country. Another favourite new dish was a clam or seafood chowder. We made two versions in the hotel, the New England one which was milk-based, and the Manhattan one which had a tomato base. I now make my own version of chowder which is always a great success in London on Thanksgiving Day. I named it after Albert!

At the Elizabeth, clams were served very simply, just steamed, and though I have always liked them that way, I longed to try and create a sauce to serve with them. It wasn't until much later, when I went to Japan, that I suddenly remembered the clams in Montreal, and the idea came to me of trying them with a black bean sauce, which I think is original.

At the Pavilion, not all the dishes were of the same high standard. As *sous-chef* in charge of the *garde manger*, one of my roles was to prepare the whale meat and whale skin salads which were served in support of the Inuits, the North American Eskimos whose way of life was under threat (and who have recently won the rights to their own homeland). The whale skin had to be cooked for hours and then required masses of seasoning as it had very little flavour. I can't say it was one of my favourite dishes.

Wild rice, hand-picked by Indians in Manitoba, was another indigenous find. Albert Schnell used it as a stuffing for Cornish hen . Adapting that recipe (see page 48), I created a dish of quail stuffed with wild rice. (Occasionally I use couscous instead, because it is more absorbent and easier to cook.)

One of my very favourite of Albert's recipes is *Crêpe sans Rival*. This is a light sweet pancake filled with *crème* >

Albert's Seafood Chowder

SERVES 4

100 g (4 oz) fillet of monkfish 100 g (4 oz) fillet of smoked haddock	Cut into dice of about 2.5 cm (1 in).
12 clams 20 mussels	Scrub and rinse under plenty of running water. Remove beards from mussels, and place mussels and clams in a large pan.

1 litre (1¾ pints) Fish Stock (see page 156)	Add 100 ml (3½ fl oz) to the pan, cover and simmer until the clams and mussels are open, a few minutes only. Remove the shells from the stock and leave to cool.
	    Strain the stock through a fine sieve and keep for later.
	    Remove the hard white tendon from the clams and the black parts from the mussels. Cut the flesh into small pieces.

30 ml (2 tablespoons) olive oil 25 g (1 oz) onion, peeled and chopped 1 small garlic clove, peeled and crushed	Sweat together in a large pot for a few minutes.
25 g (1 oz) each of thinly sliced leek and diced green pepper	Add, and cook for another 2–3 minutes. Add the rest of the stock and the strained liquor, and bring to the boil.
2 ripe tomatoes, skinned, seeded and diced a pinch of saffron (optional) 15 ml (1 tablespoon) each of finely cut parsley and chives	Add, along with the seafood dice, and heat through briefly. Serve very hot.
Garlic Croûtons (optional, see page 52) a little lightly whipped cream (optional)	Use as a garnish.

ANTON'S TIP

Use any seasonal seafood you like – oysters would be good – and alternative vegetables such as carrots.

Clams with Black Bean Sauce

SERVES 4

40 medium clams	Scrub well, then place in a suitable saucepan.

200 ml (7 fl oz) Fish Stock (see page 156)	Add to the pan, and bring to the boil. Cook until the clams open, about 2–3 minutes.
	   Remove the clams from the stock, take off and discard the top half shell, and keep the clams warm.
	   Boil to reduce the stock by half.

50 g (2 oz) each of diced red, yellow and green pepper **30 ml (2 tablespoons) finely cut spring onion** **15 ml (1 tablespoon) fermented black beans** **salt and freshly ground pepper**	Add to the reduced stock, season to taste with salt and pepper, and bring to the boil.
4 small red chilli peppers	Divide the clams between four plates, and pour the sauce and vegetables over them. Garnish with the chilli peppers.

Quails Stuffed with Wild Rice

SERVES 4   OVEN: Moderately hot, 190ºC/375ºF/Gas 5

8 quails salt and freshly ground pepper	Cut down the back with a sharp knife and remove the bones. Remove the livers and set aside. Remove the breast bones and pull out the upper thigh bone. Season with salt and pepper.
5 ml (1 teaspoon) finely chopped shallot 10 g (⅓ oz) butter livers of the quails, diced 120 g (4½ oz) cooked wild rice 20 g (¾ oz) apple, peeled and diced 40 ml (1½ fl oz) double cream 1 egg yolk a little fresh thyme	For the filling, sweat the shallot in the butter, then season the liver dice and sauté them. When cool, mix with the cooked wild rice and apple dice. Add the cream and bind with the egg yolk. Season with thyme, salt and pepper. Stuff into the quails, return the birds to their original shape, and tie with small pieces of string. Season with salt and pepper.
40 ml (1½ fl oz) olive oil	Heat in a roasting pan, put in the stuffed quails and sauté on both sides.
20 g (¾ oz) each of finely chopped carrot and celery 5 ml (1 teaspoon) finely chopped shallot 8 juniper berries	Add to the quail pan, then transfer to the preheated oven and roast until crisp, 15–20 minutes, basting constantly. Remove the quails and keep warm. Remove the fat from the roasting pan, leaving the juices.
50 ml (2 fl oz) Madeira 200 ml (7 fl oz) Brown Poultry Stock (see page 157)	Add to the juices in the pan, then boil to reduce to half the original volume.
50 ml (2 fl oz) meat glaze (optional, see Tip)	Add, bring to the boil and strain, then season with salt and pepper. Arrange the quails on a suitable dish, and cover with the finished sauce.
a few salad leaves and vegetables	Use to garnish, and serve immediately.

ANTON'S TIP

A meat glaze – *glace de viande* – is often added to sauces to give that sheen special to dishes from professional kitchens. A large quantity of brown meat stock is reduced, over a low heat, and in a succession of smaller saucepans, until it is thick and shiny and intensely flavoured. Ideally the reduction should be by nine – 10 litres reducing to one litre.

patissière, and peach or apricot slices, covered with a meringue mixture, and then put under the grill to form a glaze. The contrast between the cold pancake filling, with a hint of Kirsch, and the warm meringue is quite sublime.

With Albert's excellent tutelage, I worked my way up from *chef tournant* to *chef saucier* and then second *sous-chef*. Hardly surprising then, that I stayed on for much longer than I originally intended. Then one day he announced that I was to become his first assistant which meant that when he was away I was in charge of and responsible for 150 chefs at the age of only twenty-one. Perhaps the greatest challenge during that period was overseeing the preparation of food for the banquet of

5,000 people which was held every year. That was some experience, and luckily it went off without a mishap.

I remember it was in Montreal that I first came up with my chicken winglet idea. Generally the wing of the bird is discarded which may not be significant in the case of a couple of birds, but imagine if you were serving thousands of guests, that's an enormous amount of meat to throw away. What, I wondered, could one do with the wings? The answer I came up with was to bone, marinate and grill them. I experimented and then showed the chefs how to turn over the wing, cut off the ends and then remove the small bone. The result was a delicious bite-sized snack. Admittedly it used to take hours of fiddly work to prepare >

enough for a large party, often at the expense of a few scratched fingers, but I thought it was well worth the time considering how much money was saved. Not surprisingly, perhaps, it never became popular with the chefs!

As in all kitchens, there were chefs whose route to the kitchen came simply by chance. There was one chef in particular, whose story I love. This was Dominic, a Sicilian, who had originally come over as a bricklayer and had helped to build the hotel. Once the hotel was up he was out of a job, so he asked if they could find some work for him. He was given the role of pot-washer in the kitchens and as time went by he started chopping parsley when he had run out of pots to scrub. One day someone else arrived to wash pots and Dominic moved on, helping out elsewhere in the kitchen. To cut a long story short, after a considerable time had passed, he ended up as *chef potager*, in charge of preparing soups.

When I became *sous-chef*, Dominic came to see me each afternoon with details of what soups he had planned for the following day. Regular as clockwork, he ran through the list, pointing to the soup on the menu. One day, however, he pointed to the smoked salmon when talking about pea soup and when I pointed out his mistake, he refused to believe me. I didn't want to argue with him but afterwards went to ask the other chefs what was going on. It transpired that Dominic couldn't read or write, but rather than admit this to me, he had always asked the others tell him beforehand what was written on the menu. That day, however, he had obviously forgotten.

I was saddened that someone with the ability to prepare a choice of six to eight different soups every day and who knew exactly the right amount of soup for 5,000 or 50 people at a sitting, had never been given the opportunity to learn to read or write. But because his story shows what can be achieved against the greatest odds, I have always used him as an example when I am teaching. I truly believe it doesn't matter who you are or what you are, if you want to achieve a certain goal, you can. I believe in promoting people who are enthusiastic, even if they are currently employed cleaning the floor. Dominic, by the way, is probably still preparing his soups at the Queen Elizabeth, or has been promoted again. >

Crêpe sans Rival

SERVES 4   OVEN: Moderately hot, 200°C/400°F/Gas 6

60 g (2½ oz) plain flour 100 ml (3½ fl oz) milk	For the pancakes, place the flour in a bowl, make a well in the centre, and mix the milk in carefully until smooth.
1 egg yolk, beaten with 1 whole egg 15 ml (½ oz) caster sugar	Add and mix in well.
20 g (¾ oz) unsalted butter, melted	Add half to the batter, and mix in well. Put the remaining butter into a pancake pan and use to fry very thin pancakes – four large, or eight small. Keep warm.
200 ml (7 fl oz) Vanilla Cream, cold (see page 157) 30 g (1¼ oz) hazelnuts, finely ground 10 ml (2 teaspoons) Kirsch	For the filling, mix together. Spread the mixture thinly over the pancakes.
4 peaches, skinned, stoned and thinly sliced (raw or poached)	Divide between the two opposite ends of the pancakes, then fold the pancake over from both sides to the middle. Place on a heatproof platter.
150 ml (5 fl oz) Meringue (see page 157) 20 g (¾ oz) hazelnuts, finely ground	Mix together carefully, then pipe through a star tube on top of the pancakes. Bake in the preheated oven for 4–5 minutes until the meringue is golden brown. Serve while the pancakes and meringue are hot, but the filling is still cold.

ANTON'S TIP

A raspberry sauce, made from raspberries pushed through a sieve, and mixed with icing sugar, lemon juice and a suitable liqueur to taste, can be used as a colourful base for each pancake when serving.

Caesar Salad

SERVES 4

2 heads Cos lettuce	Remove and discard the outer green leaves and separate the well-shaped firm leaves from the heart of the lettuce. Wash and dry thoroughly, and keep in a cool place until needed.
1 small garlic clove, peeled 2 egg yolks 2 anchovies 100 ml (3½ fl oz) sherry vinegar 40 g (1½ oz) Parmesan cheese, finely grated	For the Caesar dressing, place in a blender, and blend until smooth and creamy.
200 ml (7 fl oz) olive oil 100 ml (3½ fl oz) Vegetable Stock (see page 156) salt and freshly ground pepper a drop of Worcestershire sauce	Trickle the oil into the dressing, and thin down with the stock. Season to taste with salt, pepper and Worcestershire sauce. Keep cool until needed.
1 large garlic clove, peeled and bruised 60 ml (4 tablespoons) clarified butter	For the croûtons, rub a small frying pan with the garlic, then cook in the butter over a low heat until just beginning to colour. Remove the garlic from the pan.
2 slices bread, cut into 5 mm (¼ in) cubes	Add to the garlic-flavoured butter and cook until golden brown in colour. Drain well on kitchen paper. Place back in a clean pan.
60 g (2¼ oz) Parmesan cheese, grated	Toss 20 g (¾ oz) cheese into the croûton pan while the croûtons are still hot. Heat if necessary to melt the cheese. Arrange three to four lettuce leaves on individual plates. Drizzle some of the sauce over the lettuce, along with a sprinkle of the remaining cheese. Repeat this lettuce, dressing and cheese procedure twice more, making three layers on the plates.
finely cut chives	Garnish the top layers with chives and the warm cheesy croûtons.

ANTON'S TIP

To clarify butter, cut 225 g (8 oz) unsalted butter into cubes, and melt gently Do not boil. Skim off the milky particles, and pour the yellow butter carefully through muslin into clean jars. Store in the fridge and use as required.

ANTON'S TIP

The garlic-flavoured croûtons can also be used to garnish other leaf salads – spinach with bacon, for instance – and soups.

Whilst on the subject of soups, one of the things I always feel spoils a good soup are indifferent *croûtons*. The same goes for the *croûtons* in a Caesar salad, an American speciality I encountered at this time. To serve cold, hard and tasteless *croûtons* is such a pity: they should be warm, crisp and full of flavour. When I came to create my own Caesar salad, I improved the *croûtons* by flavouring the butter with garlic and adding some grated Parmesan cheese just before serving.

I was kept so busy in Canada what with work and taking another diploma in teaching, that I had little chance to travel much, but I made one exception and that was to fly to Mexico in the summer of 1968 for the Olympic Games. I had to spend my savings on that trip, but it was definitely worthwhile. Mexico was a wonderful place. Of course it was in total contrast to where I had come from but I loved it – the climate, the people and the food. I took a bus from Mexico City to Acapulco and tasted *tortillas* and tequila with salt and limes for the first time. Most of all, I was impressed by the incredible displays of fruit: pineapples, papaya and mangoes were piled high, mounds of fragrant colour. >

The Palace Hotel in Montreux, as it was in 1969, where I worked with Franz Wild, a marvellous chef who helped me a great deal while working for my diploma.

As for the Games themselves, I enjoyed them enormously. It was the most fantastic spectacle and an impressive feat of organisation. Eating lunch near the stadium in a friend's Swiss restaurant, I remember watching with amazement as a man started eating cheese *fondue* with a spoon. He thought it was a soup! Fondue is a dish for winter, for eating in the mountains with friends, and the restaurant should never have had it on their menu in that amazing Mexican heat!

It was March 1969 when I finally left the Queen Elizabeth. Once you have worked for some time for the Hilton group, like any other group, they are keen to keep you on, and I was offered several positions as Executive Chef at other Hilton hotels in various parts of the world. I suppose I could have accepted, but I felt that at twenty-two, I was too young for the position. I wanted to go back to Switzerland to learn more, and in particular to learn about the management side of the business without which I would never be able to be my own boss.

Returning to Switzerland meant that I would have to do my national service. I should have done this when I was nineteen but work had got in the way, so I now joined a group of 400 stationed in Lucerne, all of whom had for one reason or another missed the basic 16 weeks' training. They were a real mixed bunch, and included the Swiss running champion and several professional football players.

The initial training was for sixteen to eighteen weeks after which you were supposed to return each year for two or three weeks until your fortieth birthday. Having suffered from back trouble for some years as a result of two fused vertebrae, I wasn't sure I would survive the full training, but after an initial medical, I was pronounced fit and seconded to the cycling group. Essentially this involved a lot of hard work pedalling heavy army bikes up and down the hills with a rucksack full of equipment on my back, but it turned out to be quite fun nevertheless. In the evenings I

was put in the kitchen to peel potatoes.

The chef was by trade a cheese-maker, but he performed his role with great care, making sure that every recipe was followed just so. After a few days on site, he put me on breakfast duty but unfortunately forgot to tell me. That night I went to bed, in a room shared with twenty other men, quite unaware that at five the next morning the night guard would be expecting to find a helmet propped against the end of my bed, as a sign to wake me early, in good time to prepare breakfast.

When the night guard arrived, finding no helmet out, he proceeded to wake each sleeper, one by one. There was a lot of angry grumbling and swearing, but failing to discover the chef, the poor guard ended up cooking the breakfast himself. This went on for a couple of nights until eventually I was handed a note explaining that I should have been on breakfast rota.

After four weeks' basic training, I had another medical and this time they agreed that my back was indeed not strong enough, so I was declared unfit but, in common with all those who cannot complete their service, I continued to pay a special military tax until I was forty.

It was some relief to be able to get on with my life again and to start my new job as *chef tournant* at the Palace Hotel in Montreux. This was a couple of steps down in the kitchen hierarchy, but a necessary one if I was to work towards my *Chef de Cuisine Diplômé*, the highest culinary award in Switzerland. The kitchen brigade of twenty-five was run by Franz Wild, a marvellous chef, who gave me a great deal of help in working for my diploma. On my days off I worked at the local butcher to learn more about meat. I did my research thoroughly from visiting the abbatoir at five a.m., to learning how to bone the animal. One of the most important things I was taught was how to avoid any wastage, a skill that is particularly useful as meat becomes more expensive.

By contrast I also went to Zürich to learn the techniques of sugar-pulling and -blowing under Willy Pfund, one of Switzerland's greatest masters in that extraordinary art. At first the hot sugar burns, but gradually your hands become used to the heat and with practice you can create the most wonderful sculptures. Sadly, it is an art that is often forgotten as it takes more time and money than most kitchens can afford.

Franz Wild was classically trained, and could sometimes lose his temper, but most of the time he was very good-natured and soon became a great friend. We learnt to keep quiet and keep out of his way when he was in a bad mood. When one of the chefs had really upset him, his face and neck would flush a deep red as he started to shout. Sometimes he got so beside himself he would whip off his chef's hat and jump up and down on it with rage.

But when he relaxed and started to talk about food he was mesmerising. He had an extraordinary ability of being able to describe dishes in such detail that you could almost see them before you, actually smell and feel them. It was he who really taught me how to handle food, and, most importantly, how to keep tasting all the time. I always remember the way he used to taste a sauce. This big man with his large, smiling face would delicately dip just the tip of his little finger in the sauce, just so. Then very quickly he sucked the sauce like a bird before pulling his finger out of his mouth with a flourish! It was a great performance.

His was a friendly kitchen and I sensed, coming back to Europe after three years abroad, that my status had significantly changed. It felt good to have the juniors coming up and asking me what it had been like in Canada or wanting advice about their careers.

On one occasion, a young man I particularly liked, an Englishman called Rex, asked me for 300 francs to contribute towards the fees for a cookery course. That was quite a lot of money in those days, but I could see the course would be good for his career, so I agreed and sadly that was the last I saw of him or the money. Or so I thought. It was ten years later, when I was at the Dorchester, that the phone rang one day. I answered it and immediately recognised the voice. It was Rex. He had been working in Africa when he read about me in some catering magazine, and had resolved that as soon as he had saved the money, he was going to repay me. He didn't pay me any interest, but at least I got it back!

At the end of the season, although I was sad to leave Montreux, I was looking forward to spending the winter at the famous Palace Hotel in St Moritz. As I walked up the slope, the hotel looked quite beautiful, lying in the deep snow, surrounded by mountains. It was a marvellous hotel with an excellent reputation, and it was thanks to the personal recommendations given by Franz, an old friend of the chef at the Palace, that I got the job as first *chef tournant*.

Monsieur Defrance, the French chef, was eighty-seven years old and as a young man had worked as *commis saucier* with the great Escoffier when he was *Chef de Cuisine* at the Savoy. Sometimes he would remember those days, his eyes glistening as he relived the past. Escoffier, he said, was gentle, yet fully master of the kitchen. Though Defrance was only a *commis*, he was often asked to prepare recipes that Escoffier was testing.

I DO BELIEVE CHILDREN SHOULD BE ENCOURAGED INTO THE KITCHEN TO LEARN ABOUT FOOD WHEN THEY ARE YOUNG. THAT WAY THEY GET A FEEL FOR THE TEXTURE OF RAW AND COOKED FOOD, AND GAIN A SENSE OF WHAT FLAVOURS COMPLEMENT EACH OTHER AND WHAT COMBINATIONS WILL OR WON'T WORK.

Despite his age, Monsieur Defrance was full of *joie de vivre*. He used to drink a bottle of champagne a day, and was always the first to arrive and the last to leave. One of his more eccentric habits was gathering the chefs' knives which he collected to sell when he visited Paris! Of course we never complained because he was such a kind old man and anyway, what would have been the point, he was a law unto himself.

Understandably Monsieur Defrance no longer cooked, but he used to write all the menus, and sometimes, when the champagne and his eighty-seven years caught up with him, he fell asleep as he worked. As first *chef tournant* I often worked near his office and used to quietly close the door so that he could sleep for an hour or so. It made little difference to the brigade as the *sous-chef* Monsieur Cola, a youthful sixty-five, used to run the kitchen, taking all the day-to-day decisions.

After a couple of weeks at the Palace, Monsieur Defrance asked me if I would prepare lunch for him. He wanted lamb chops and a few vegetables. Of course I was honoured to have been asked, but I was even more pleased when he asked me again the following day. Thereafter, until I left, it was always my job. Another dish that I learned to cook there, and still cook today, was a roast chicken decorated with gold leaf.

Looking back on those kitchens now, I am amazed by the quantities of butter, cream, *foie gras* and truffles that were consumed. However much I used for garnishing, I was always told to add more. One New Year's Eve, we actually served up 50 kilos (some 111 lb) of Beluga caviar! For someone who had worked with René Rastello's strict budgets, this was quite an eye-opener.

Monsieur Cola was a true Italian, very kind, with a warm heart and a hot temper. He was very emotional and at Christmas he used to suffer at having to be alone, away from his home and his family. During food service he was liable to lose self-control. The tension would overcome him and he would scream at everyone, usually taking his temper out on the waiters. But, after the service, it all blew over. He calmed down immediately and would often come up, put his arms round my shoulders, and we would walk off together happily chatting as though nothing had happened.

At that time there was undoubtedly more tension between waiters and chefs. These days there is generally more teamwork and understanding, but then it wasn't unusual for an irate chef to take his anger out on a waiter, sometimes hurling more than just abuse.

That was something we all had to just accept, as we did the traditional kitchen hierarchy. There was no means of becoming a chef other than working your way up from the bottom. Those grand old men, with their famous bad tempers and red faces, were the kings of their domain, able to bully the new (and not so new) boys to their hearts' content. None of us liked it much, but it was the only way of learning.

Waiters and junior kitchen staff there had to share bedrooms, sometimes sleeping six or eight to a room. It was normal, though, for one of them to be getting up at five-thirty in time for the breakfast shift; this would wake the others who might have only got in at two or three in the morning after the night shift. Luckily I had a very nice room just outside the hotel which I shared with only one other. My free time and nights were very much more peaceful.

Monsieur Defrance, chef at the Palace Hotel in St Moritz, who had once worked with Escoffier at the Savoy in London. Although eighty-seven years old, he still enjoyed a bottle of champagne per day.

Roast Chicken with Gold Leaf

SERVES 4   OVEN: Moderately hot, 200°C/400°F/Gas 6

1 maize-fed chicken, about 1.4 kg (3 lb) salt and freshly ground pepper	Clean and season inside and outside.
1 garlic clove, lightly crushed 2 sprigs fresh rosemary	Place in the cavity, and put the bird in a greased roasting tin.
40 ml (1½ fl oz) olive oil	Brush over the chicken, then roast in the preheated oven for about 20 minutes per 450 g (1 lb). Cover with oiled greaseproof paper or foil if the breast is becoming too brown. Remove from the oven and allow to rest for a few minutes.
sheets of edible gold leaf	Place neatly over the breast of the chicken before carving. Eat warm.

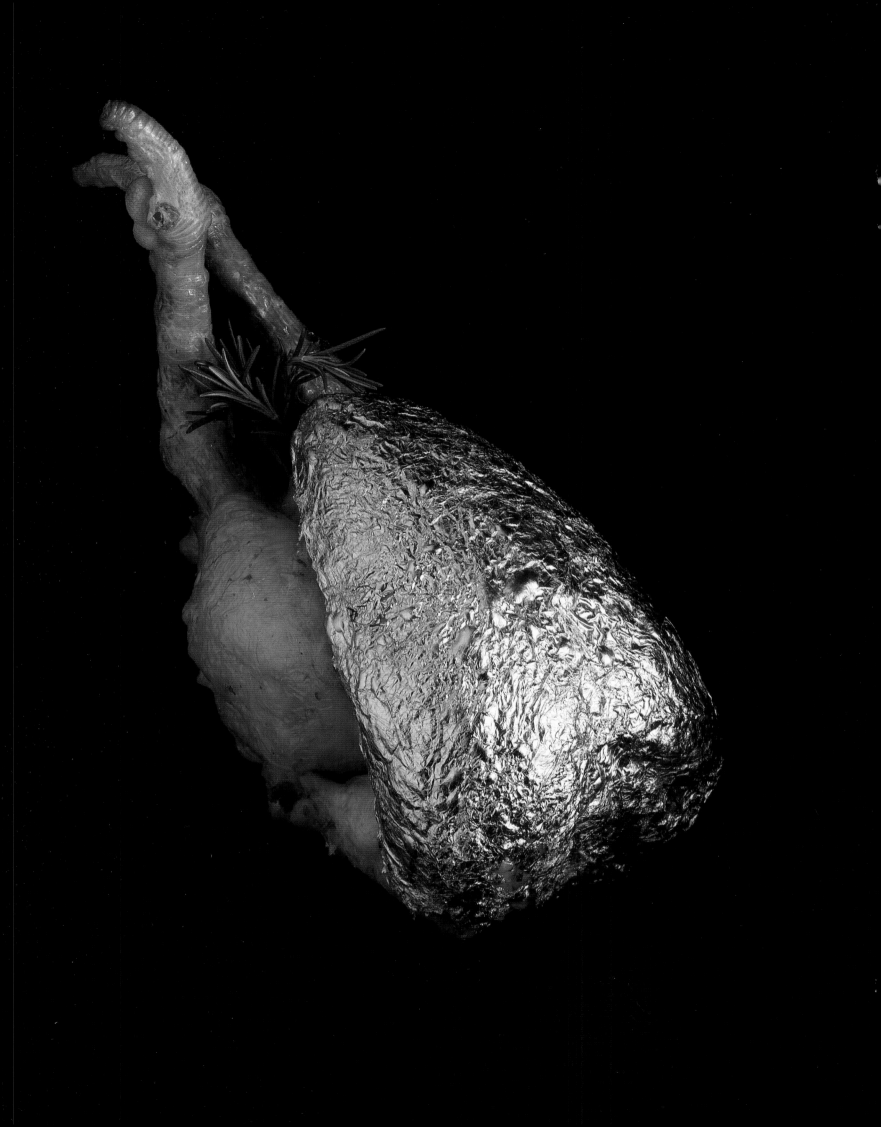

Chapter Four

A Journey in Japan

As usual, I had looked for and found the next adventure in my culinary education. It was that December in St Moritz that the letter arrived confirming my appointment as *sous-chef* at the Swiss Pavilion for Expo '70 in Japan, a country whose way of life had long intrigued me.

After leaving the Palace, I set about looking for material about Japan. I read all the guide books I could find and even started to learn some basics of the language. I was all but ready to leave when Swissair, contracted to run the Pavilion by the Swiss Government, asked me to take over as Executive Chef, since they had been unable to find a suitable chef for the role.

It was incredibly good luck and a great challenge, and I was only too aware that even though I was only twenty-three, I couldn't afford to make any mistakes. My way of dealing with my anxiety was to devote myself to the preparations, going through the various menus with a fine toothcomb to be absolutely certain they contained no errors.

On the plane to Osaka, my concentration on matters culinary faltered, for it was then that I met Kathrin, the head housekeeper for the Swiss Pavilion. She was to become my wife three years later.

I took with me ten Swiss chefs who were to work in a team with thirty-five local chefs from some of the best hotels in Japan. On that first morning, as we assembled in the kitchen, it was immediately apparent that I was one of the youngest there! The Japanese culture is of course highly respectful of age and hierarchy, and I realised that I was going to have to be extremely diplomatic so as not to offend any sensibilities, not least since a good number of the Japanese chefs were already in their mid-thirties and early-forties.

Determined to make things run as smoothly as possible, I had arranged for all the recipes to be translated from German into English and then reproduced alongside photographs of the dishes. So once we had introduced ourselves, the Japanese chefs gathered with their pencils and notebooks to take notes in Japanese to keep for reference as they prepared Swiss dishes like *Raclette Montagnard*, *Eminçé de Veau Zürichoise* or *Rösti*.

Luckily I had learnt how to exchange greetings in Japanese, and though I could hardly strike up a conversation, I was soon able to communicate quite well, at least in the kitchen. I think that helped smooth the way, and once the daily regime had been established, everyone settled in. The Japanese were soon turning *Rösti* with chopsticks as though it was their own national dish. Chopsticks, I soon learnt, were extraordinarily versatile!

Yet, despite all my efforts, there were some difficulties I could not have foreseen. The Japanese *chef garde-manger* came up to me one afternoon looking very puzzled. He wasn't happy with the way the salad dressing had turned out and asked me to taste it. It was too thick, so I checked the recipe in case there had been some mistake in the translation. No, that was fine and the chef promised me he had followed the recipe instructions to the letter. He went off to try again but returned with the same results. We wouldn't work out what was going

Japanese Omelette

SERVES 4

8 eggs, beaten **a little Vegetable Stock (see page156)** **15 ml (1 tablespoon) light soy sauce** **salt**	Place in a bowl and mix, seasoning to taste with salt.
60 ml (4 tablespoons) finely grated *daikon* radish	Moisten and flavour with a few extra drops of soy sauce. Set aside. Heat a rectangular Japanese egg pan over medium heat until hot.
vegetable oil	Lightly wipe the pan with a cloth swab moistened with oil. Pour about two-thirds of the egg mixture into the pan and tilt so it spreads evenly. When it begins to bubble around the edges, tilt the pan up towards you and, with a pair of chopsticks, roll the egg layer towards you. With the oil swab, oil the pan surface again, and push the egg roll back away from you. Add the second third of the egg mixture and tilt the pan as before, lifting the edge of the rolled omelette so that the raw mixture runs underneath. When that in turns starts to set, roll as before. Oil again, pour in the last third of the mixture, cook and roll in the same way. Remove from the pan and wrap in bamboo mat (if available). Press gently and let rest for a minute to shape. Unwrap and slice crosswise into 5 cm (2 in) rounds. Place two slices on each serving plate, and garnish with a mound of soy-flavoured *daikon*.

ANTON'S TIP

For variation, garden peas, puréed spinach, shreds of *nori* seaweed, prawns or eel can be added to the omelette mix.

A postcard showing the spectacular sight of 30,000 light bulbs outside the Swiss Pavilion, at Expo '70 in Osaka.

wrong, so step by step we examined the recipe in great detail, and only after a lengthy discussion did we discover the answer. Japanese eggs were a bit larger than those in Switzerland! Simple. All we needed to do was reduce the quantities from six eggs to four. The only trouble was that as far as the Japanese chef was concerned the recipe said six, and it was very difficult to persuade him that we would have to change the ingredients. As I grew to know and increasingly respect the Japanese, I realised that this inflexibility was not unusual.

I learnt another way of using those slightly larger eggs from one of the local chefs. Basically an omelette – but often flavoured in a Japanese way with soy sauce and seaweed – it is cooked and presented in an unusual and very appealing fashion.

That same chef and his colleagues also introduced me to *tofu*, soya bean curd, and that was later to inspire me to create a lighter mayonnaise, using *tofu* instead of egg yolks, as a dressing for a Japanese-inspired soya bean salad.

I found it enormously rewarding to work with the Japanese. They are great team players, very supportive, rallying round if any extra help is needed, and they are very fair. But one of the most immediately noticeable bonuses of working with Japanese chefs is that they hardly ever

shout! It was, sadly, the Swiss chefs who more often than not failed to come up to scratch.

Cultural differences did, however, create problems in getting around town. Osaka is an industrial town, not so exciting a place as Tokyo, but it was nevertheless the busiest city I had ever been in, and the rush hour was unbelievable, with passengers being forced on to trains by special attendants. At first we found it almost impossible to hire a taxi. The moment the driver realised we were not Japanese, rather than admitting he could not understand us, he would drive off before we could say a word. Since >

Spring Salad

SERVES 4

200 g (7 oz) soya beans, soaked in cold water overnight 10 ml (1 dessertspoon) vegetable oil	Drain then cook until soft in water to cover plus the oil. In the pressure cooker this takes around 30 minutes; on the stove, about 1½ hours. Strain and leave to cool.
250 g (9 oz) small-leaved spinach, de-stalked 50 g (2 oz) dandelion leaves	Wash and shake off excess moisture. Cut the dandelion leaves into strips.
2 bunches radishes, about 300 g (11 oz) in total 1 bunch chives	Wash then trim and slice the radishes finely. Cut the chives finely.
200 g (7 oz) silken tofu, chopped 60 ml (4 tablespoons) Vegetable Stock (see page 156) juice of 1 lemon 15 ml (1 tablespoon) Dijon mustard 15–30 ml (1–2 tablespoons) soy sauce, to taste	For the tofu mayonnaise, put all the ingredients together into the blender and blend well – it takes 1 minute or so to emulsify. Put the soya beans in a dish and mix with the tofu mayonnaise. Add the spinach, dandelion, radishes and chives and mix together gently.
salt and freshly ground pepper	Season to taste and serve immediately.

ANTON'S TIP

Although good by itself, this salad is delicious as an accompaniment to baked jacket potatoes.

Vegetable Tempura

SERVES 4

15 ml (1 tablespoon) Dijon mustard 50 ml (2 fl oz) lemon juice 150 ml (5 fl oz) olive oil 1 bunch watercress, leaves only, chopped 20 g (¾ oz) flat parsley, finely cut 30 ml (2 tablespoons) finely cut chives 2 pieces spring onion, finely cut 2 hard-boiled quail's eggs, roughly chopped 4 tomatoes, skinned, seeded and diced salt and freshly ground pepper	To make the dipping sauce, mix together and season to taste with salt and pepper.
400 g (14 oz) mixed small vegetables (mushrooms, carrots, radishes, sweetcorn, parsley sprigs, etc)	Prepare the vegetables, peeling and wiping clean if necessary, but leaving stalks on if appropriate.
75 g (3 oz) plain flour mixed with 25 g (1 oz) cornflour	Dust the vegetables with 15 ml (1 tablespoon) of the mixed flour, and salt to taste. Place the rest of the flour in a bowl and make a well in the centre.
1 egg, beaten 100 ml (3½ fl oz) iced water	Add to the well, along with a pinch of salt, and mix together to a thin batter.
fresh corn oil for deep-frying	Place in a suitable pan (you could use a wok) and heat to around 160°C (325°F). Dip the vegetables, a few at a time, into the batter, holding by the stalk, or using a fork, skewer or chopsticks. Gently drop into the oil and pre-cook for about 1 minute, then remove and drain well on kitchen paper. This can be done in advance, see Tip. Re-fry the vegetables in hot oil – at about 170°C (340°F) – for a few minutes more until crisp and golden. Drain well. Serve the tempura hot with the cold sauce.

ANTON'S TIP

Do not put too many items in the deep-frying oil at one time. Do them in batches.

The first frying can be done well in advance; the second frying should take place just before serving.

Other vegetables, cut in small pieces, can be used, as can shrimps, prawns, pieces of squid and small white fish.

we were living in a special village outside Osaka with all the other foreign representatives, we had in fact learnt how to give the address and directions in Japanese, but we rarely got the chance. In the end we had to almost hijack a taxi, climbing in the moment the driver had pulled up!

One of the first things I do in a new country is to visit the local food markets. I like to know exactly what kinds of fruit and vegetables are available and to look at the quality of the local meat, fish and poultry. Food differs from area to area because of the climate, the soil and how it is cultivated, and therefore may well need to be cooked differently. It has always been my philosophy that a chef should be constantly in touch with his growers and suppliers. As I

would never bring anything with me to a job in a new country except my knives, so I always insist on buying my ingredients from the local shops.

You might think this is obvious, but I feel there are far too many chefs who don't bother to regularly go round the markets themselves and consequently miss some of the freshest and most interesting ingredients. I remember once in South Africa returning from a shopping expedition with a lot of local produce which the resident chefs had never seen before. Thinking that I had imported such fresh vegetables, they were genuinely surprised that they were regularly sold in the market.

In Japan the markets were quite unlike anything I had

With the kitchen brigade of the Swiss Pavilion. Cuno Blattner, the general manager, is to my left.

ever seen. Melons, for example, were individually sold in a special presentation box and cost from £25 up to £50 each! The packaging was taken to extraordinary lengths. Peas were sold loose, wrapped in a small sausage of plastic film, and strawberries were arranged, in four neat rows, twelve to a box.

There were familiar and unfamiliar vegetables on sale, but all were of extraordinarily high quality. Later I learnt how to make the light batter for *tempura*, deep-fried morsels of those wonderful baby vegetables, or of seafood, which are dipped into a tangy sauce.

I arranged to visit the world-famous *kobe* beef farms where, I discovered, they massage the cattle for twenty minutes every day with *saké*. This keeps the flesh tender whilst the daily drink of beer gives it a wonderful flavour. The farm was extremely modern, very clean and the cattle were allowed to spend six months of the year in the field and the remaining six months indoors.

In Osaka I was inevitably attracted by the fish market. The colours of those magnificent deep-sea fish and the variety of species are quite astounding. To ensure total freshness, fish were sold alive and kept in great tanks >

Tuna Tataki with Sesame Cucumber Noodles

SERVES 4

1 cucumber	Peel, cut in half lengthwise and remove the seeds. Slice lengthwise into spaghetti-shaped strips with the aid of a mandoline, and place in a colander.
salt and freshly ground pepper	Sprinkle 5 ml (1 teaspoon) salt over the cucumber 'spaghetti' and leave for about 30 minutes.

400 g (14 oz) piece of tuna tail
40 ml (1½ fl oz) sesame oil
	Meanwhile season the piece of tuna with salt and pepper, and rub with a little of the oil. Sear all sides either over a direct flame or in a heavy non-stick pan or griddle.
	    Cool, then place in the fridge.
	    Rinse the cucumber in cold water and squeeze dry.

juice of 2 limes **finely grated zest of 1 lime** **30 ml (2 tablespoons) light soy sauce** **15 ml (1 tablespoon) sesame seeds, roasted**	Mix together with the remaining oil, and toss with the cucumber. Season to taste with salt and pepper. Take a fork and twist the cucumber 'spaghetti' around it, then arrange on the plates. Top with thin slices of the tuna.
1 spring onion, chopped **a few coriander leaves** **1 red chilli pepper, seeded and finely sliced (optional)**	Use to garnish the tuna.

where people could pick them out individually. They were then scooped out and placed in a plastic container filled with water.

Whilst there one morning, I had a memorable breakfast – a bowl of steaming fish broth with noodles and some of the most sumptuous and fresh seafood I have ever tasted. It was simple fare – a Japanese equivalent of the onion soup served at the old Les Halles in Paris, I suppose – but was very welcome on a cool morning and very delicious! I later developed my own version.

I stood for a long time at the fish market just watching the fishmongers at work. They had two knives, one for *sushi*, one for filleting. They chopped and sliced with great professionalism. It was quite different from the very basic techniques of a traditional European fishmonger. The Japanese approach is far more dedicated, and it was a real joy to see them working.

The same care and dedication to the work was evident amongst the Japanese chefs in my kitchen. I remember watching two of them chopping a pile of parsley. Not content with just getting the job done, they were having a competition to see who could chop faster! And on one particularly hectic day, one chef, Mogi San, cooked *Rösti*

non-stop for five or six hours in three or four small pans. He worked uncomplainingly, determined to meet the sudden increase in demand, turning the *Rösti* incredibly fast with his chopsticks, and regularly wiping the steam from his glasses.

It was marvellous to have that kind of enthusiasm around me, particularly as we were cooking hundreds of meals a day, and for many celebrities including Marlon Brando, Peter Ustinov, Mary Hopkins and Sasha Distel. Of all the restaurants, ours was one of the most popular, and would also be sought out by people like Marie Helvin and Pierre Cardin, there for the fashion shows.

Sometimes I asked Japanese chefs to cook for the European staff which gave me a wonderful opportunity to stand back and watch as they worked. They produced ingredients and dishes I had only heard of before like *shabu shabu* (a beef broth), *sushi* and *sashimi*. I was incredibly excited as this time our roles were reversed. They were the masters and I was the apprentice, watching always, then gradually learning from them how to handle the fish for *sashimi* and *sushi* – the wafer-thin slices of pink salmon, the fine threads of spring onion and translu- >

Seafood Noodle Pot

SERVES 4

150 g (5 oz) Chinese egg or glass noodles	Blanch in boiling water to soften, then drain.
150 g (5 oz) squid, cleaned and sliced into rings or squares 150 g (5 oz) fresh monkfish fillet, thinly sliced 150 g (5 oz) fresh salmon fillet, thinly sliced 120 g (4½ oz) cooked mussels	Divide between two individual heatproof serving pots. Add the noodles.
100 g (4 oz) thin leeks 100 g (4 oz) carrots, peeled 100 g (4 oz) shiitake mushrooms	Trim as appropriate. Cut the leeks diagonally into thin slices; score channels along the carrots with a cannelle knife, then slice. Divide all the vegetables between the two pots.
400 ml (14 fl oz) White Poultry Stock (see page156) salt and freshly ground pepper	Bring to the boil, taste for seasoning, and divide between the pots. Heat the pots on top of the stove until the stock is simmering again.
15 ml (1 tablespoon) finely cut spring onion or seeded red chilli pepper 15 ml (1 tablespoon) fresh coriander or parsley leaves	Add to the pots, divide between four dishes, and serve straightaway, piping hot.

ANTON'S TIP

This is a very versatile dish, as it can be made with whatever seafood or vegetable is available in the market. Shrimps, prawns oysters, scallops or white fish would be delicious; mangetout, broccoli or green or red peppers would add colour and flavour.

Sushi

MAKES ABOUT 30 PIECES

120 ml (4 fl oz) Japanese rice vinegar 30 g (1¼ oz) caster sugar salt to taste	For the sushi rice dressing, mix together and leave to steep overnight.
450 g (1 lb) short-grain rice	Wash well under cold running water for 5 minutes. Leave to drain for at least 30 minutes. Place in a heavy-bottomed pan and add 850 ml (1½ pints) cold water. Bring slowly to the boil. Increase the heat to high, cover and boil for 3 minutes. Reduce the heat to medium for 5 minutes. Reduce the heat to low, and cook for 5 minutes. Off the heat, place a piece of muslin or a clean teatowel under the lid and leave for 15 minutes. Pour sushi dressing to taste over the hot rice. Use a rice paddle to mix the dressing and rice in a cutting motion . Fan the rice to cool it rapidly to body temperature. Mound it in a bowl and cover with a damp cloth.
100 g (4 oz) each of three types of fresh seafood, prepared (fish filleted, squid skinned, molluscs shelled etc)	Seafood for sushi should be the finest and freshest; it can be pre-cooked or uncooked. Cut the fish portions into pieces, some thin slices, some small chunks.
15 ml (1 tablespoon) *wasabi* (green horseradish)	The simplest sushi are made from spoonfuls of rice formed into little blocks in a suitable mould. Spread a little *wasabi* on a piece of seafood, and press a block of rice on top. Shape more sushi in a similar fashion.
several sheets of *nori* (dried laver) cucumber, peeled and seeded and green and red pepper strips sesame seeds finely cut chives red lumpfish roe	Have ready as 'wrapper' and garnish, if making more elaborate sushi. Either wrap the slices of raw fish around a little rice and garnish attractively, or surround chunks of fish and vegetable with rice and then a strip of *nori* to make pretty shapes as in the photograph. Roll some in cut chives or sesame seeds.
250 ml (8 fl oz) dark soy sauce 25 ml (1 fl oz) *mirin* (sweetened rice wine)	Simmer together in a small pan for 2–3 minutes, then cool. Serve as a dipping sauce for the sushi.

cent slices of ginger. *Sushi* – raw fish with vinegared rice – is a dish I now make and serve, and which has become amazingly popular on the menu at Mosimann's.

This was the first time I had encountered raw fish as a major ingredient in a cuisine. I *had* eaten raw fish before, and once I became used to the unusual texture and taste, I fell in love with it. It revolutionised the way I thought about food and its preparation.

Seafood of course is very healthy, and to serve it uncooked and unadulterated, seemed honest, and a homage to its beauty and delicacy. Many of my recipes now utilise raw seafood – the scallop *tartare*, for instance – but of course it has to be extremely fresh.

There is nothing fresher than the food used in Japanese recipes (except perhaps that used in Chinese ones). I was inspired by their philosophy of using the freshest ingredients, not necessarily the most expensive, and then being as creative as they could be with what they had. It is a >

Years after Expo, I was able to return to Osaka, to teach the principles of Cuisine Naturelle at the famous Tsuji cookery school. One dish was the tofu dressing, inspired by my first visit to Japan.

simple but effective approach to cooking, and was undoubtedly one of the essential inspirations of my *Cuisine Naturelle*.

Two of the dishes that I have since adapted for a Western palate are salmon *sashimi* and tuna *tataki*. My versions differ from the Japanese in that the fish, sauce and garnishes are served together rather than in separate dishes. I like the idea of using tuna for the *tataki* as I felt this was such an underrated fish. Usually it comes so overcooked that the texture is more like cotton wool than fresh fish, but with this way of cooking, the outsides of the fillet are briefly seared so that the inside remains moist and tender (see page 63).

The Pavilion closed in September with the news that we had won first prize for having the cleanest kitchen and another gold medal for being the best restaurant of Expo '70. It was a wonderful end to the season, but rather than heading straight home, I stayed on tor a while.

I took the bullet train from Osaka to Tokyo and was totally exhilarated by the experience. In Tokyo I had to visit the fish market, the largest in the world, and the largest tuna market in the world too. That was quite staggering. Early in the morning, just around dawn, the noise is deafening as the auction takes place. Buyers cut a piece from the tuna to check the colour of the meat before entering the furious bidding.

While in Tokyo I wanted to try as many restaurants as possible. I enjoyed the whole presentation, from the decor of the restaurants to the way the food is prepared and served in front of the customer. The striving for simplicity, the belief that less is more, was worlds away from everything I had ever encountered. I learnt a great deal about presentation and the use of colour in food from the Japanese. Just a few colours, I realised, could produce a powerful effect, as in the *tofu* dish overleaf which I later developed.

It was the first time, too, that I had seen such a high >

Scallop Tartare

SERVES 4

250 g (9 oz) shelled scallops, trimmed	Chop the white flesh finely with a sharp knife, and place in a bowl. Save the roe (coral) for another dish.
15 ml (1 tablespoon) lemon juice 15 ml (1 tablespoon) cold-pressed olive oil salt and freshly ground white pepper	Mix in, and season carefully with salt and white pepper. 　Shape into four rounds and arrange on individual plates. Make a dent in the middle of each round.
4 quail's egg yolks	Carefully place a quail's egg yolk in each dent.
15 ml (1 tablespoon) each of finely cut chives, coarsely cracked black peppercorns, cracked red peppercorns and chopped capers 2 shallots, peeled and finely chopped	Use to garnish the plate imaginatively.

Steamed Tofu with Young Leeks and Wakame Vinaigrette

SERVES 4

400–500 g (14–18 oz) fresh silken tofu	Remove from its water and wrap in a clean cloth. Press with a plate and stand for an hour to remove excess water. Cut into four squares.
1 packet *wakame* (dried seaweed)	Rinse with water to get rid of the salt, then soak in fresh cold water until soft, about 20–30 minutes. Drain and cut into rough pieces.
about 450 g (1 lb) young leeks	Wash, top and tail, then cut into 5 cm (2 in) lengths, avoiding the very green parts.
about 2 litres (3½ pints) Vegetable Stock (see page 156) or water	Bring to the boil and blanch the leeks for 2–3 minutes until just tender. Add the *wakame* pieces for about 30 seconds. Drain well, and place in a bowl.
60 g (2½ oz) carrots, trimmed and peeled	Cut into very fine dice (*brunoise*), and add to the leeks.
30 ml (2 tablespoons) each of cider vinegar, light soy sauce and walnut oil 50 ml (2 fl oz) light olive oil	Mix together for the vinaigrette, and pour over the leeks, *wakame* and carrot.

8 caps of medium shiitake mushrooms, cleaned
5 ml (1 teaspoon) peeled strips of fresh ginger
salt and freshly ground pepper
	Mix together and season to taste.
	    Place the four pieces of tofu in the upper part of a steamer, and divide the mushroom mixture between them. Steam for 5–6 minutes until the tofu is heated through in the centre.
	    Divide the leek, wakame and vinaigrette mixture between four plates, and top with the tofu and mushrooms.

about 15 ml (1 tablespoon) finely cut chives or spring onions	Sprinkle over the tofu and serve.

standard in food carving. The Japanese specialised in ice carvings and butter sculpture, producing some breathtaking buffet centrepieces. They are world champions in ice work, capable of producing carvings as high as a house, and in most hotels they had a special decorating department with professional chefs who are trained solely to prepare themed parties. A banquet for a visiting British dignitary might have as its centrepiece an ice carving of Big Ben, several feet high.

On the way back Europe I stopped off in Thailand where they also specialise in carving, but using vegetables and fruit which they sculpt with astonishing skill, creating birds, fish and flowers in great detail from something as ordinary as a carrot. This was the first time I had tried Thai food and I loved it, particularly the way they combine fiery spices with fragrant herbs like lemongrass and citrus leaves. Here, as in Japan, I tried to get off the beaten track as much as possible, to make sure I discovered the way people really lived, not just what they thought the tourist was interested in seeing. After spending some time talking to local people and travelling around the beautiful countryside, it was soon time to set off home.

The trip had been a great success, and it ended with an offer to become head chef in a major hotel in Tokyo. It seemed like an offer I could not refuse, but I knew that I was still not ready.

Chapter Five

Back Home Again

MUCH AS I HAD LOVED BEING ABROAD, IT FELT GOOD TO BE BACK HOME IN SWITZERLAND, AND I WAS LOOKING FORWARD TO SEEING AGAIN THE LONG SHADOWS OF MY BELOVED MOUNTAINS.

HAVING HEARD THAT A FORMER COLLEAGUE WAS NOW HEAD CHEF AT THE PALACE HOTEL IN LAUSANNE, I CONTACTED HIM TO SEE IF THERE WERE A SUITABLE POSITION FOR ME. THIS MAN, MONSIEUR FULROTH, HAD BEEN HENRI DESSIBOURG'S *SOUS-CHEF* AT THE PALACE HOTEL IN VILLARS. THERE I HAD FOUND HIS MANNER SOMETIMES A LITTLE HARSH, BUT NOW I FELT THINGS WOULD BE DIFFERENT. I WAS OLDER AND MORE EXPERIENCED, AND I WAS CONFIDENT THAT, DESPITE THE UNGENTLE MANNER, MONSIEUR FULROTH KNEW EXACTLY WHAT HE WAS DOING. HE WAS A TRUE PROFESSIONAL AND IN FULL CONTROL OF THE KITCHEN.

FROM THE BEGINNING, EACH STAGE OF MY CAREER WAS PLANNED WITH ONE GOAL IN MIND, AND IN ORDER TO SUCCEED I COULD NOT WASTE TIME WORKING IN A BADLY ORGANISED KITCHEN. I WANTED TO WORK ONLY WHERE I FELT I COULD LEARN, AND SO I PREFERRED TO TAKE A TEMPORARY DROP IN SALARY OR STATUS IN ORDER TO WORK UNDER A GOOD CHEF OR IN A NEW POSITION BECAUSE I WAS AWARE THAT, IN THE LONG RUN, THE EXPERIENCE WOULD PAY DIVIDENDS.

I started work in November as *chef entremétier*, and my role was to help out occasionally on various sections as needed. As the system in Lausanne was very much the same as that at the Palace in Villars, and the chefs were a friendly lot, I quickly found my way around. For the first weeks I concentrated on the vegetable section, a very important but often overlooked position.

The kitchen was, as I had expected, well run and efficient, and the only problem was that familiar one of the Chef being rather mean with the staff food. Those of us who worked in the kitchen were generally all right, but the waiters would often complain that they were only given leftovers and not very much of them. It came as no surprise to discover after a few days that there was a thriving barter system in action, with waiters swapping drinks for food on the sly.

I was now preparing for the Chef de Cuisine Diplômé, and I spent some time planning where I should spend the next season. I wanted somewhere that would offer the experience I needed for the diploma and after some searching I found myself a position as *chef garde-manger*, in charge of the cold larder, at the Palace Hotel in Lucerne for the summer.

Otto Schlegel, the *Chef de Cuisine*, was one of the most respected chefs in the country, and had given the hotel and restaurant an excellent reputation. For the last quarter century he had spent the summer season at the Palace in Lucerne and the winter at the Palace in Gstaad. He was a warm, fatherly figure, who took good care of his chefs, making sure they were content and offering advice where he could, though again he had little time for waiters.

At this point in his career, he was no longer creating the innovative dishes of his youth, but was concentrating on bringing out the very best from each one of his twenty chefs. He also insisted, most importantly, on only using the very finest ingredients. He would wander round the kitchen, checking that all was well. Nothing less than top quality would satisfy him. For the chef, everything had tobe '*très, très soigné*', just so. From him I learned one of

The Palace Hotel, Lucerne, where I worked with Otto Schlegel, one of the most respected chefs in the country, and Jürg Reinshagen.

LIKE MOST OF MY PEERS I BELIEVE STRONGLY

THAT FOOD SHOULD BE AS FRESH AND

LIGHTLY COOKED AS POSSIBLE AND THAT

SAUCES, FAR FROM BEING A HEAVY PORRIDGE OF

his specialities, the veal dish following.

Every summer Herbert von Karajan came to Lucerne to conduct, and on these occasions he always stayed at the Palace. Naturally the chef was determined to offer the great conductor the finest dishes, and von Karajan's favourites were calf's head with herb vinaigrette and poached turbot. Each March when Otto Schlegel came down from Gstaad, one of the very first things he did was to visit the butcher's to remind him not to forget von Karajan's calf which was needed in August. The poor animal, I remember, wasn't even born at this stage.

A few days before von Karajan was due, the calf's head would be delivered to the kitchen where it was soaked for twenty-four hours in cold running water just to make sure that it was as white as possible. Then we would shave all the hairs off the head with a sharp knife. This was only the beginning of what was an enormous and lengthy procedure. On the day that the calf's head was to be served all the chefs were required to arrive an hour early for work. We had first to take the flesh off the bone and then blanch it, cut it up into small pieces and finally simmer it. This was quite tricky, and every ten minutes the chef would be round to check all was going according to plan. Meanwhile the delicate vinaigrette dressing was prepared and >

Emincé de Veau Lucernoise

SERVES 4

600 g (1 lb, 5oz) trimmed veal fillet, cut in fine slices salt and freshly ground white pepper 50 g (2 oz) unsalted butter	Season the veal then carefully sauté the slices in the butter without browning. Let the meat drain in a sieve.
50 g (2 oz) each of small chanterelles, *cèpes* and button mushrooms	Wash the chanterelles and *cèpes* thoroughly, and then slice the *cèpes*. Slice the button mushrooms finely.
½ shallot, peeled and finely chopped	Sweat in the butter remaining in the veal pan with the mushrooms for a few minutes.
200 ml (7 fl oz) white wine	Add to the pan and boil to reduce a little.
200 ml (7 fl oz) Brown Veal Stock (see page 157)	Add, and bring to the boil.
150 ml (5 fl oz) double cream	Add, and reduce by half.
15 ml (1 tablespoon) chopped parsley	Add with the meat. Season with salt and pepper.
30 ml (2 tablespoons) raisins, soaked in a little white wine 8 walnuts, shelled and halved	Use a garnish, and serve immediately.

ANTON'S TIP

Oyster mushrooms may also be used, if *cèpes* and chanterelles are not in season, or soaked, dried mushrooms.

To make this dish even more interesting, sliced calf's kidneys can be added.

LOUR, MUST BE REDUCED FROM THE COOKING JUICES . . .

Mignons of Venison with Parsley Purée

SERVES 4

250 g (9 oz) parsley, without stalks	Make the parsley purée first. Wash well and steam for a few minutes. Liquidise without any water.
50 ml (2 fl oz) double cream salt and freshly ground pepper	Add, and season with salt and pepper. Keep to one side.
12 × 40 g (1½ oz) mignons of venison, well trimmed	Season on both sides.
70 g (2¾ oz) butter	Melt 30 g (1¼ oz) of the butter in a pan and gently sauté the mignons to pink – about 2 minutes on each side. Keep hot. Remove the butter from the pan, and keep it.
200 ml (7 fl oz) red wine (Burgundy)	Add to the meat juices in the pan, and boil to reduce by half.
400 ml (14 fl oz) reduced Game Stock (see Tip)	Add, and allow to reduce a little, then stir in the remaining butter, a little at a time. Strain and season with salt and pepper.
400 g (14 oz) small chanterelles, well cleaned 1 shallot, peeled and very finely chopped	Sauté in the reserved venison butter for a few minutes. Season with salt and pepper. 　Place the well seasoned sauce on serving plates, and arrange the mignons on top. Garnish with the chanterelles, and serve the parsley purée separately.

ANTON'S TIP

To make a game stock, follow the instructions for Brown Poultry or Veal Stock on page 157, but using finely chopped game bones and trimmings. Add 4–5 juniper berries with the diced vegetables, and 300 ml (10 fl oz) white wine with the first water addition.

had to be tasted by Monsieur Schlegel.

I'll never forget the moment when the head waiter came rushing downstairs and announced '*Il est là.*' You could feel the tension rise. The chef was almost beside himself as the calf's head was dressed on a magnificent silver dish, which had to be polished like a mirror. All the chefs stood round to watch the show and add the final garnishes before Monsieur Schlegel pronounced the dish ready. Finally, the waiter would pick it up and carry the feast upstairs. One year, however, the waiter was so nervous of the chef that in his fear, he slipped, and dropped the whole dish on the floor. The resultant pandemonium just goes to show what comes of being so perfectionist. Herbert von Karajan always seemed to enjoy the dish immensely, though I'm sure he never knew just how much work went into its preparation.

Monsieur Schlegel loved fishing and often spent his day off with his rod and line usually catching three or four fish, which he would show off when he came back to the hotel

in the evening. If there was one big one and three tiddlers, he would put his hand into his bucket of water and proudly pull out the large fish, then put it back again into the water. Then, rather than show the small ones, he'd pull out the large one again three more times. I've no idea whether he thought he'd actually fooled us!

When it came to giving us days off he never worked out the rota in advance, but would just run his finger down the list of names and then look in the kitchen and if you happened to be passing he'd say 'OK, you. You can take tomorrow off.' On one occasion when my *commis* hadn't had his day off for a couple of weeks, I waited until I saw the chef go into his office and pull out the list. Quickly I fetched my *commis*.

'Just go in there ask him something, anything, and I bet you he'll give you a day off!' I said, and indeed he did.

Working with Otto Schlegel was always a pleasure and I returned to the Palace every summer for the next three years, working my way through the kitchen as *chef rôtis-*

seur, *chef saucier* and finally *sous-chef*.

Over those years I also made some very good friends. We used to go swimming, kick a football about, and spent hours playing cards. I shared a room on the sixth floor with a wonderful view over the lake. One night there I remember seeing a shadow fall across the window and when I looked up there was this chef waving at me through the window. He had got so drunk that he had climbed outside and was walking along the guttering!

In between seasons I filled in time by doing various courses. The first autumn I learnt how to sculpt butter, and then I decided to take a cookery teaching certificate.

In the winter I went up to St Moritz to work as *chef restaurateur* under Pierre Gilgen at the Kulm Hotel, which had been recommended by a number of friends. This was a kitchen where only the best was good enough. For me it was sheer pleasure to be able to cook with table wine and table butter, not the cheaper and inferior versions commonly used.

We used a lot of local game, especially venison, and we cooked it in a variety of ways – roast, braised, steaks and mignons quickly pan-fried and served with wild mushrooms.

One of the major benefits of the Kulm for me was the opportunity of working with the pastry chef, François Gatti. He came from the Italian part of Switzerland, and was then about seventy-five years old. He taught me a great deal about pastry, and the two tarts here owe much to him.

Another aspect of the Kulm I particularly enjoyed was the kitchen itself. Unlike the usual sunless basement, this kitchen had large windows through which you could see the day passing and the darkness of night fall.

As *chef restaurateur*, I was responsible for *à la carte* cooking which I really enjoyed, because you never knew what the next order would be and consequently had to be constantly at the ready and very flexible. To be able to do this you must have all the ingredients already prepared, of which perhaps the most important are the different basic sauces. The only way I knew of ensuring that these were of the finest quality, clear and shiny, with a good flavour, was to cook them myself, and at least twice a week I would do so. I then stored the sauces in the fridge in large, empty marmalade containers.

After a few days I came downstairs one morning to discover that a major proportion of one sauce had vanished. Nobody had any idea what could have happened, but I had my suspicions.

I went over to see Gemma, the staff cook. Gemma was a wonderful Italian *Mama* and she loved everybody. She

The Kulm Hotel, St Moritz, where I stayed for several winter seasons from 1971 with Pierre Gilgen, Head Chef. Here I was taught a great deal by the pastry chef, Francois Gatti.

was a big lady with an even bigger heart, and had worked for the last twenty-five years at the Kulm Hotel. She used to call me *Dottore* (professor) because, unlike her, I used to plan everything I cooked very carefully. I always laid out my ingredients precisely, the salt, the pepper, the herbs, everything in dishes ready for use. Each morning Gemma would be downstairs early, cooking her minestrone and pasta for the staff lunch. Of course she wanted only the best for everybody, so in went more butter and more olive oil without a thought for the expense.

As I went up to talk to her, I could see she was stirring a large pan of rabbit and vegetables, simmering in a delicious rich brown sauce. With just one look and one sniff, I knew that this was my sauce. But when I asked her if she had seen my sauce, she was adamant in her denials. I said nothing more, but the next day the level in the container had sunk again. The same happened the following day. I realised that although I didn't want to cause a fuss, because I liked Gemma and also knew she was good friends with the head chef, Mr Gilgen, I was going to have to take some kind of action. I resorted to more basic tactics. The next time I made my sauces I took them upstairs to my room at the end of the day and there they stayed beside my bed until the next morning. The bedroom was so cold, I didn't need a fridge anyway!

Gemma soon realised that something was wrong. '*No che più salsa, Antonio?*' How did I manage without sauces, she wondered. 'Don't worry,' I told her, 'I know where I can get some.' And that was that. She had to make her own then! But nothing was ever said out loud. I was glad because it was a particularly friendly kitchen. We all loved working there and would be up by seven in the morning and in the kitchen by eight. After a late night, often still half asleep, the heat from the oil-fired stoves really hit you.

Every morning, on getting up, I promised myself I'd

Hard work, but worthwhile.

have an early night. By ten o'clock at night, with work slowly finishing, someone would always come along, though, and suggest going out. However strong my resolution, somehow or other I'd end up agreeing to go out just for one coffee. Then before I knew where I was just one cup had turned into another and a game of cards, and then suddenly it was two in the morning. We were all good friends, working and living so closely together, and it went on like that for the whole season!

In the end I developed a wonderful way of getting through the day without feeling totally exhausted. During the afternoon break I would go out for a little fresh air, then have a three- to five-minute cat nap. When I woke, I felt completely restored and ready to take on anything. It's a habit I've never given up and I've found it incredibly useful.

After much hard work and many long days, I got my head chef's diploma in December 1972 at the age of twenty-five. I was actually too young to sit the exams as you were supposed to have worked a certain number of years after your apprenticeship. Even when they calculated the total number of days I'd worked – seven years, two months and twenty-five days – it still wasn't quite enough. >

Swiss Apple Tart

MAKES 1 × 20 CM (8 IN) TART, or 4 SMALL TARTS   OVEN: Moderately hot, 190ºC/375ºF/Gas 5

150 g (5 oz) plain flour, sifted	For the sweet pastry, place in a mound on a clean work surface, and make a well in the centre.
75 g (3 oz) unsalted butter, cut into cubes 30 g (1¼ oz) icing sugar, sifted 1 egg yolk finely grated rind of ½ lemon	Add to the well in the flour, and work together, then gradually incorporate the flour until a smooth paste is formed. Roll into a ball, and rest for at least 20–30 minutes in the fridge. Roll out and use to line the greased tart tin or tins. Leave in a cool place for about 20–30 minutes.
30 g (1¼ oz) raisins 30 ml (2 tablespoons) Calvados	Soak the raisins in half the Calvados.
25 g (1 oz) unsalted butter 75 g (3 oz) brown sugar	To begin the filling, heat together in a heavy-bottomed frying pan until the sugar dissolves.
4 cooking apples, peeled and cored	Cut each apple into thin wedges. Add to the butter and sugar in the pan and sauté quickly for about 5 minutes. Flame with the remaining Calvados, then remove pan from the heat and leave to cool.
80 g (3¼ oz) unsalted butter 80 g (3¼ oz) caster sugar	For the frangipane, whisk together until light and fluffy.
1 large egg, beaten 100 g (4 oz) ground almonds 30 g (1¼ oz) plain flour 15 ml (1 tablespoon) milk	Fold into the butter and sugar. Spread the frangipane over the tart base, and smooth the surface. Arrange the apple slices and juices over the top. Spoon the raisins and Calvados into the middle. Bake in the preheated oven for about 30–35 minutes until cooked and lightly golden brown in colour. (The small tarts will only need about 20–30 minutes.) Remove from the oven and transfer tin(s) and contents to a wire rack. Turn out of tin(s).
icing sugar (optional)	Dust over tart and plate to serve.

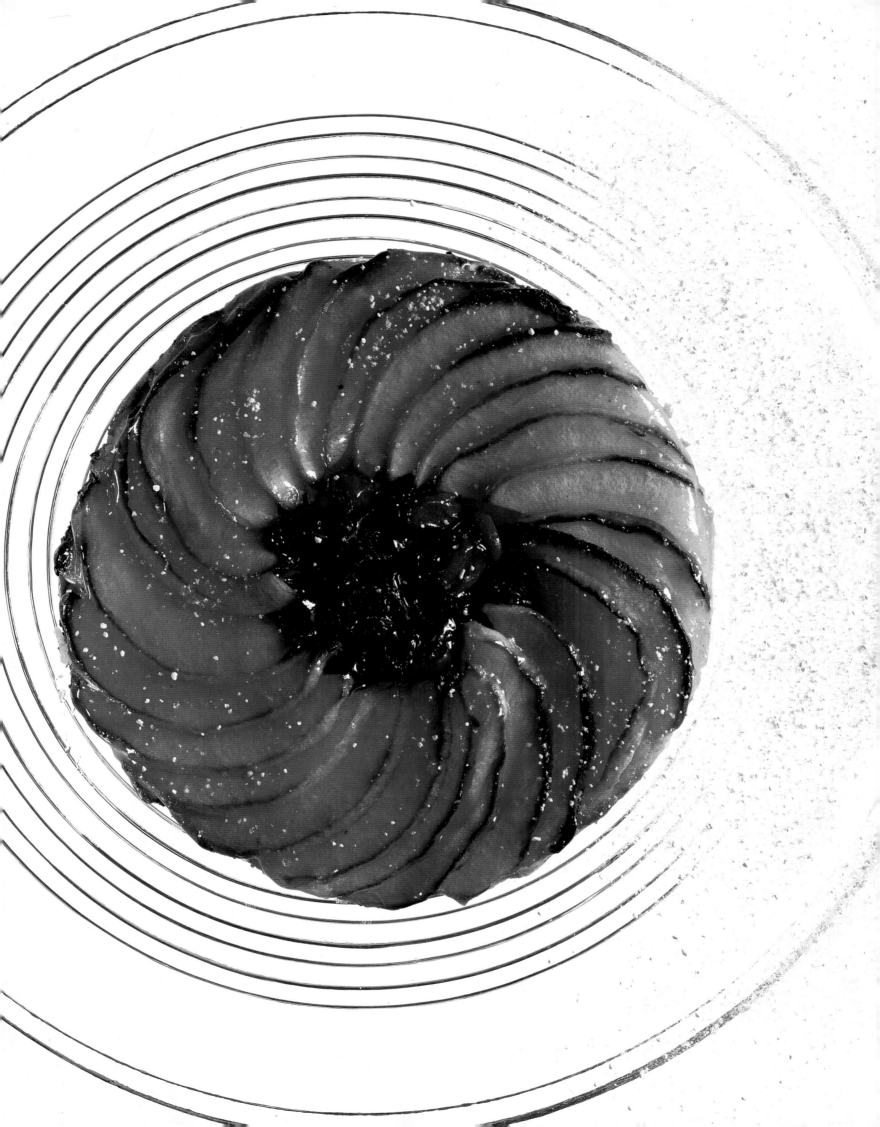

Luckily they agreed to make an exception because of my background, and I was allowed to take the exams. At that time the failure rate was 60 per cent so I was extremely proud to have passed, particularly since I was the youngest person ever to have done so.

The following year, 1973, I won first prize in the National Cookery Competition but otherwise the seasons passed as usual in Lucerne and St Moritz. In between I filled in with some teaching which I really enjoyed and found enormously rewarding. It was marvellous to be able to help bring out the potential in these young chefs. I also managed to find time to get married . . .

When I returned to Lucerne the following April it was again as *sous-chef*. Work went as usual until one day in June the Head Chef had a heart attack and was taken to hospital. As his first assistant, I was called into the office by the general manager, Herr Jürg Reinshagen, and told

quite simply that now I was to take over. I couldn't believe what I was hearing, but he was adamant. Mr Schlegel was now in hospital and my age, he said, was immaterial.

'If you can't do it now,' he said, 'you will never be able to.' Looking back, I know he was right, not just for then, but in general. As long as you have the basic *feel*, the drive and the determination, age does not matter. When he said that, I realised I was ready. I had covered every area of the kitchen, and I felt confident about myself and my abilities. Most of all, I was determined to put everything I had into the task.

I had to take over immediately, and quickly found there was an awful lot of work to do. My days got longer and longer as I had to put together menus, organise days off and make sure that I gave my very best. Once I had mastered the day-to-day management of the kitchen, I began looking at ways in which I could make some improve- >

Swiss William Pear Tart

MAKES 1 × 20 CM (8 IN) TART, or 4 SMALL TARTS   OVEN: Moderate, 180°C/350°F/Gas 4

ANTON'S TIP
Instead of the chocolate, you could use a dark fruit purée as garnish (see page 82).

1 quantity Sweet Pastry (see page 78) 25 g (1 oz) plain flour	Roll out, using the flour, on a work surface. Line a greased flan ring (or rings) resting on a baking sheet with the pastry, and prick the base with a fork. Leave to rest in a cool place for about 30 minutes. Line the pastry shell(s) with a piece of foil or greaseproof paper. Three-quarters fill with baking beans and bake blind for about 10 minutes in the preheated oven. Remove and cool.
8 ripe William pears, peeled and cored	Roughly grate into a bowl.
finely grated zest of 1 orange and 1 lemon 30 g (1¼ oz) soft brown sugar a pinch of ground cinnamon 50 g (2 oz) fresh cake or brioche crumbs 50 g (2 oz) raisins 25 ml (1 fl oz) walnut oil	Add to the pears in the bowl and mix well. Remove the baking beans and foil or paper from the blind-baked pastry shell(s). Fill with the pear mixture, spreading it evenly.
40 g (1½ oz) brown sugar 100 ml (3½ fl oz) double cream	Sprinkle with the brown sugar, and cover with the cream, then bake for 30 minutes (20 for the small tarts) in the oven at the same temperature. Loosen the sides of the flan ring(s), and leave to cool. The flan will set more firmly as it cools.
Vanilla Cream (see page 157)	Make and place a portion on each serving plate.
a little dark chocolate, melted	Spoon on to the vanilla cream and draw a cocktail stick or skewer through to make a swirl. Add a piece of tart and serve.

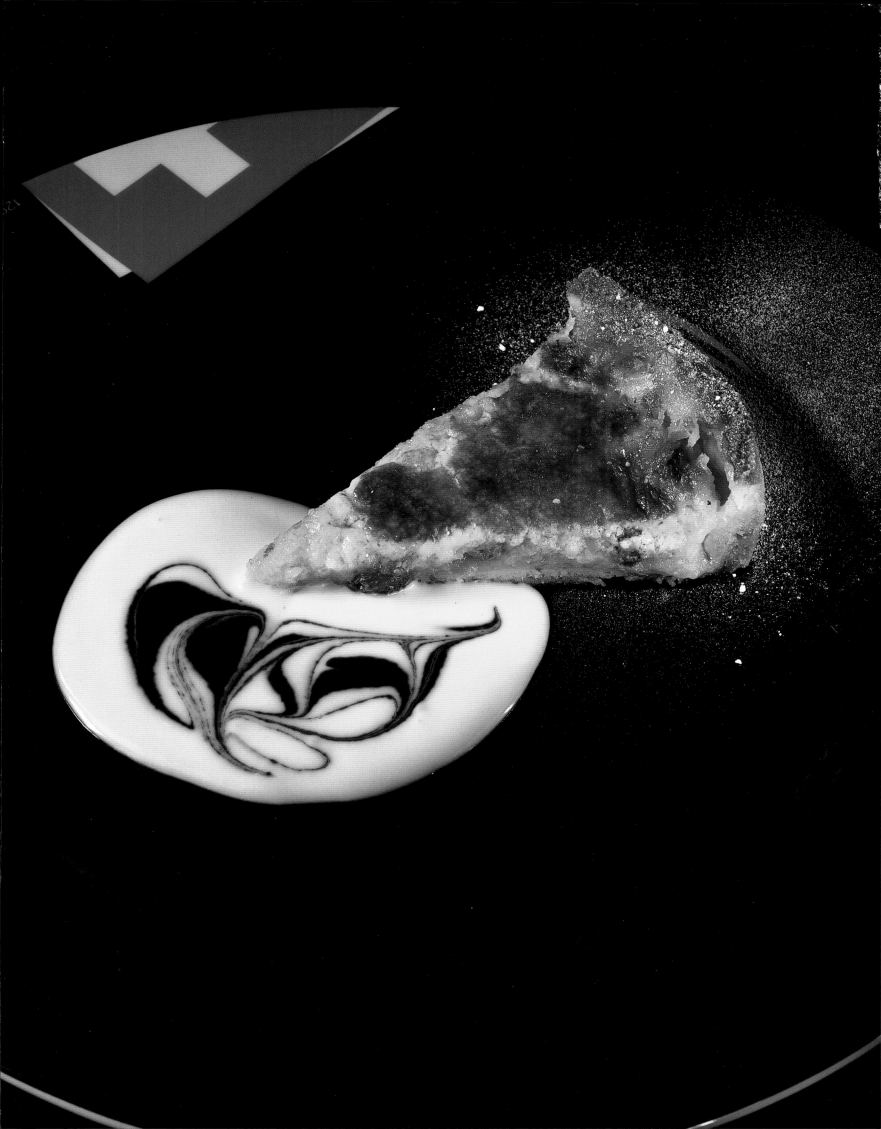

Symphony of Fruit Purées

SERVES 4

250 g (9 oz) apples, peeled, cored and sliced juice of 1 lemon a little caster sugar a little apple juice	Cook the apples until soft in a minimum amount of water with a little lemon juice and sugar. Allow to cool and strain through a fine sieve. Thin down with a little apple juice if necessary. Chill.
200 g (7 oz) blackcurrants, cleaned and stemmed 100 ml (3½ fl oz) mineral water	Bring blackcurrants to the boil in a very little water, lemon juice and sugar. Allow to cool, then purée and strain through a fine sieve. Thin down if necessary with a little of the mineral water. Chill.
1 large mango, peeled and stoned	Purée in the liquidiser. Strain and thin down if necessary with a little mineral water. Chill.
1 paw-paw, peeled and seeded 200 g (7 oz) kiwi fruit, peeled 200 g (7 oz) raspberries, cleaned	Separately, purée, strain and thin down as for the mango. Chill. To serve, put a scoop of each cold purée into four large soup plates, arranging them around the plate with the blackcurrant purée in the middle.
20 ml (4 teaspoons) natural yoghurt	Place a teaspoonful on top of each scoop of blackcurrant purée. Keeping the plate level, tap it firmly on a solid surface covered with a cloth. Take a cocktail stick and draw a continuous spiral round the purées (starting from the yoghurt).
wild strawberries or raspberries tiny sprigs of mint	Use as a garnish.

ments. Twenty-five years with no change was a long time.

Mr Schlegel was away for the rest of the season (and, happily, he recovered), but this left me in charge for four months. As Acting Head Chef, I had to restrain myself from making all the alterations I would have wanted had it been my own kitchen. Nevertheless, I did introduce some lighter dishes and more salads to the menu. One of my innovations at this time was the dessert 'soup' of fruit purées. Europe has a tradition of fruit soups anyway, but this I thought was one step better – as well as a creative and economical way of using fruits slightly too ripe to serve in other dishes.

At the end of the summer, I left Lucerne intending to spend some time in Zürich with Adelrich Furrer, one of the greatest *chefs traiteur* I had ever met. He was a charming strong-minded man and famous for his elaborate butter sculptures which formed the centrepieces of his magnificent cold buffets. He was a true artist. Adelrich was now getting on in years and he no longer worked in hotels except when invited as a guest chef to prepare buffets for grand openings. Instead he was responsible for creating new recipes for the Swiss association of mushroom growers.

Having heard about his skills, I arranged to spend some time with him, learning as much as I could. Adelrich was a fellow Swiss, liked my eagerness, and kindly took me under his wing. We became very good friends despite the difference in our ages. A few weeks later, I received a letter from him asking whether I would be interested in joining the team at the Dorchester Hotel in London. The *Maître Chef des Cuisines* for the last twenty-five years, Eugène Käufeler, he wrote, was an old friend (they had been apprentices together in Zürich), and he had asked Adelrich if he could suggest a suitable successor. Initially the appointment would be as executive *sous-chef*, taking over as Executive Chef in six months' time. It was an >

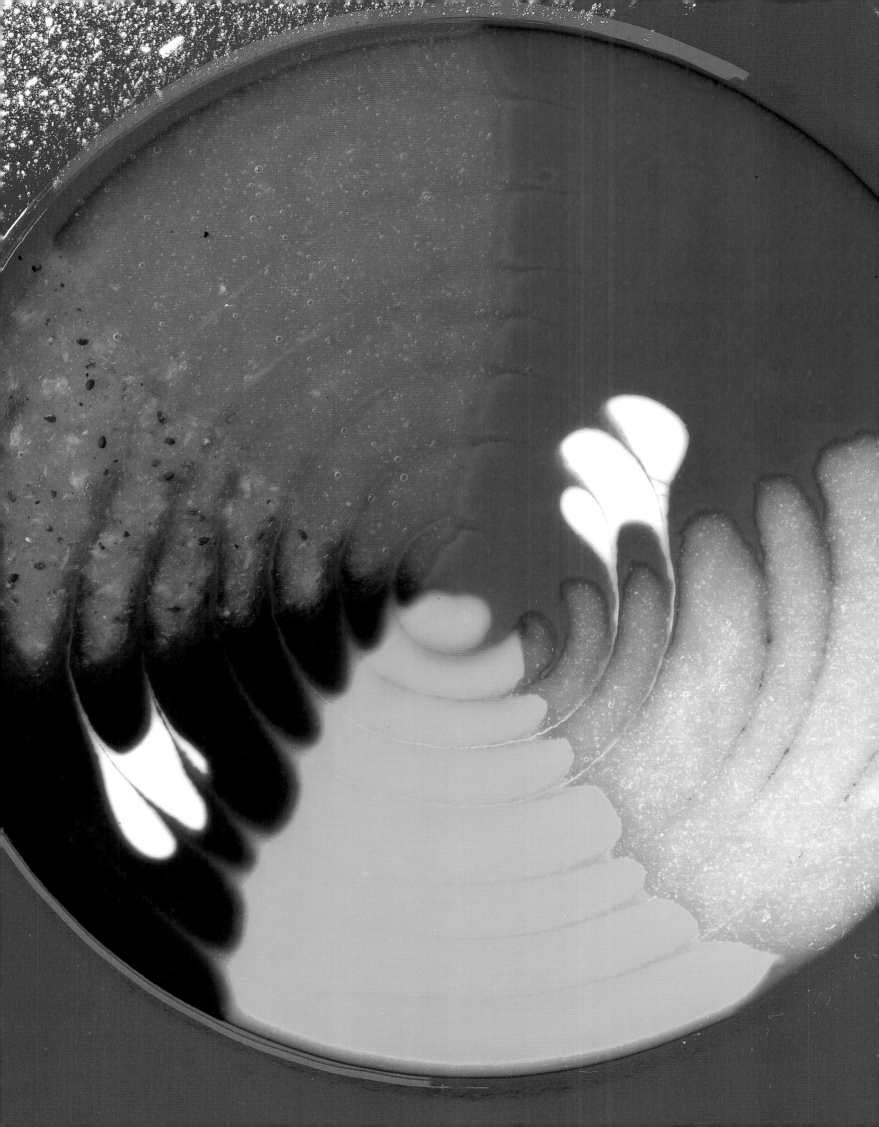

Many years later, during a short break from filming in Switzerland, I was photographed wearing traditional Bernese costume.

MUCH AS I LOVED THE DISCIPLINE AND THE PHYSICAL FEELING OF

WELL-BEING AND PERSONAL SATISFACTION THAT CAME FROM TRAINING

AND KEEPING FIT, I KNEW THAT IT WOULD NEVER MEAN AS MUCH TO ME AS

FOOD. SPORT COULD BE MY HOBBY, BUT COOKING HAD TO BE MY LIVING.

I TRULY BELIEVE IT DOESN'T MATTER WHO YOU ARE OR WHAT YOU ARE,

IF YOU WANT TO ACHIEVE A CERTAIN GOAL, YOU CAN.

incredible feeling. The Dorchester in London! I had to read the letter several times. This was a job I would love to do. I sent off my papers, they were approved, and I was to fly over to London in February for an interview.

Since I was not due, in any event, to join the hotel until the following summer, I arranged with Otto Schlegel to spend the winter with him at the Palace Hotel in Gstaad, working as an ordinary *commis pâtissier*. Although François Gatti had taught me a lot, I had never worked on this section, one that Head Chefs often know little about. Having always had a sweet tooth, it was also a position I was looking forward to! When I was younger, a considerable amount of pocket money disappeared in bars of chocolate which we often ate for picnics, simply putting a few slabs into a bread roll. And of course with my mother's thorough teaching, I had quickly learnt to appreciate the delights of strawberry and other *gâteaux*.

In Gstaad I concentrated on learning the skills of pastry-making, which I consider essential for any serious chef. We made our own cakes: the famous Swiss carrot cake, which originated in the canton of Aargau, and the delicious cherry tart, *Zuger Kirschtorte*. We also made a variety of ices and sorbets as well as doing a good deal of sugar work which I thoroughly enjoyed. I learned how to handle chocolate, a very delicate substance, which can easily be ruined by overheating it only slightly.

The Palace Hotel in Gstaad, where I worked as the most junior pastry chef in the winter of 1974.

February was cold and bright when I left Gstaad for London to meet the Dorchester managing director, Robin Oldland, David Petrie, the food and beverage manager, and Mr Käufeler himself. Sitting in the back of a black taxi, coming in from Heathrow, the sky was leaden and a cold rain fell. It was my first visit to London but there was no time to do any sight-seeing, I had only time to go straight to the interview.

Most of the questions, and there were dozens of them, were put by David Petrie, who struck me immediately as everything I had imagined a true Englishman to be – always extremely proper, yet with a schoolboy sense of humour. I couldn't help noticing, on his desk, a photograph of his labrador wearing his master's spectacles. Years later the story went round that even when on holi- >

Chocolate Chip Ice Cream

SERVES 10

350 g (12 oz) bitter or dark chocolate	Chop and melt 250 g (9 oz) of the chocolate in a bowl over a bain-marie of hot water.

250 ml (9 fl oz) milk **250 ml (9 fl oz) double cream** **½ vanilla pod, split**	Heat together gently, then bring to the boil.

4 egg yolks **25 g (1 oz) caster sugar**	Whisk together until starting to go pale. Slowly whisk the boiling milk into the egg yolks, then return the mixture to the saucepan, and cook over a low heat, stirring all the time, until the mixture coats the back of the spoon. Strain the custard into the melted chocolate and blend well, then leave to cool. Place in a mould or container and freeze for 2–3 hours. When thick and half-frozen, take out, place in the blender, and process to a smooth cold mixture. Chop the remaining chocolate very finely and stir in. Return to the container and the freezer for another 1–2 hours until frozen.

ANTON'S TIP

You can serve the ice cream layered (at the last minute) between home-made chocolate biscuits or waffles. Another idea is to cut out circles of chocolate. Melt a good dark chocolate gently (perhaps with a little orange liqueur) and then pour it out on to a cool working surface (a piece of marble). When the chocolate has cooled a little, mark with a round pastry cutter, then leave to set completely. Remove the circles carefully.

day, David would lie on the beach in his suit, his briefcase beside him in the sand! And once, when we spent two days together in Paris, David, who had worked there at the Ritz just after the war, was mystified that we couldn't find our way around the city using his old 1947 map. Extraordinary!

At the first interview we had so many things to discuss that we actually ran out time, and as I had booked my return flight to Switzerland, there was nothing for it but to arrange a second meeting three weeks later. This time we covered everything after which I signed the contract and flew back to Switzerland.

Peppered Pineapple with Vanilla Ice Cream

SERVES 4

4 egg yolks 90 g (3½ oz) caster sugar	To make the ice cream, whisk together well in a bowl.
250 ml (8 fl oz) milk 250 ml (8 fl oz) double cream	Heat together until hot, and gradually add to the yolks. Put the mixture into a saucepan.
½ vanilla pod, cut lengthwise	Add, and bring the mixture to just below boiling point, stirring constantly, until the mixture coats the back of the wooden spoon or spatula. Remove immediately from the heat and allow to cool in a cold bain-marie, stirring occasionally. Strain through a fine sieve and freeze in the usual way. (This quantity is enough for ten people; you will have some left over.)
100 g (4 oz) caster sugar	Make the sauce next. Melt in a pan and let it become slightly brown (caramel).
50 ml (2 fl oz) each of fresh orange juice and Crème de Cacao 20 ml (¾ fl oz) lemon juice	Add, and simmer gently to reduce a little.
30 g (1¼ oz) unsalted butter	Meanwhile, melt in a small pan and allow to brown a little. Add to the sauce.
finely cut zest of ½ orange	Blanch and add as garnish to the sauce. Keep the sauce to one side.
1 pineapple (about 300 g/10 oz)	To prepare the pineapple and finish the dish, peel the fruit and cut into slices of about 1 cm (½ in) thick. Remove the middle core.
a little freshly ground black pepper	Sprinkle over the pineapple slices.
40 g (1½ oz) unsalted butter 25 ml (1 fl oz) Crème de Cacao	Heat the butter in a pan, add the pineapple slices, and flame with the Crème de Cacao. Add the sauce and heat gently. To serve, divide the pineapple slices between four plates and arrange an oval of ice cream in the middle of each slice. Pour the hot sauce over the ice cream and serve immediately.

Chapter Six

An Interlude in Northern Europe

BACK IN GSTAAD, THE SEASON WAS DRAWING TO A CLOSE, AND I DECIDED TO SPEND THE NEXT FEW MONTHS TRAVELLING. THERE WERE STILL SO MANY COUNTRIES TO VISIT, PLACES TO SEE, RESTAURANTS TO EAT IN AND DISHES TO SAMPLE. I THOUGHT NOW WAS SENSIBLE, AS THERE PROBABLY WOULDN'T BE MUCH FREE TIME ONCE I WAS IN LONDON!

I HAD NEVER BEEN TO SCANDINAVIA, AND A FRIEND, JOSEF HILGER, WHO HAD BEEN MY *COMMIS DE CUISINE* IN MONTREAL, HAD BECOME *SOUS-CHEF* AT THE GRAND HOTEL IN STOCKHOLM. THIS SEEMED AN IDEAL OPPORTUNITY TO VISIT HIM AND SPEND SOME TIME IN THE KITCHENS THERE, AND ALSO TO FIND OUT ABOUT SCANDINAVIAN CUISINE AT FIRST HAND. I WAS PARTICULARLY KEEN TO GO TO SWEDEN BECAUSE I WANTED TO SEE HOW THEY PREPARED AND COOKED FISH, ESPECIALLY ALL THOSE HERRING DISHES.

THE GRAND WAS A WONDERFUL OLD HOTEL, WITH A GREAT NAME, AND IT WAS A LOVELY PLACE TO WORK AND STAY. IT WAS OLD-FASHIONED IN MANY WAYS — IN ITS INTERIOR DESIGN, IN ITS KITCHEN LAYOUT AND EQUIPMENT, AND THE MANAGEMENT ITSELF — BUT STILL ENJOYED A REPUTATION SECOND TO NONE. THE KITCHEN WAS ORGANISED ON CLASSICAL LINES TOO, BUT THAT WORKED WELL, AND I WAS PLEASED TO HAVE THE CHANCE TO SEE HOW AN OPERATION LIKE THIS FUNCTIONED BEFORE GOING TO THE DORCHESTER.

MOST OF MY TIME EVERY DAY WAS SPENT IN THE COLD KITCHEN WHERE I PREPARED herring and other fish for *smörgåsbord*. This is Sweden's major contribution to international cuisine, and usually means an 'open' or 'cold table', a buffet in other words. The tradition of *smörgåsbord* reached its heyday towards the end of the nineteenth century, and the Grand still nodded towards that time.

A normal *smörgåsbord* buffet has a general pattern to it, with types of food in groups: salty fish like herring and anchovies at one end of the table, the dishes perhaps set into ice, then other fish dishes such as salmon, then cold meats, salads, cheeses, with perhaps a section of hot dishes at the other end of the table. Eating from a *smörgåsbord* also has its traditions. You start at the herring end, taking a little of each of the dishes – there could be at least six different types on display – then come back later for a selection of tastes from the other food groups. It is a delightful way of eating, and I enjoyed working on that fish section very much.

I learned an enormous amount about herring, the fish that had been partly responsible for my coming to Sweden. Herring dishes abound in the cuisines of northern Europe, because they were once so plentiful in the waters of the North Atlantic and in the Baltic. In Sweden they still eat a great deal of the fish, salted, lightly pickled, soused,

smoked (as buckling), and fried. The herring of the Baltic are slightly smaller than those of the Atlantic side of the country, and in Sweden they can be subjected to a form of fermentation, to become a great delicacy known as *Surströmming*.

At the Grand, there were any number of herring recipes which I found most inspiring. One dish I later created was a *matjes* or 'maiden' herring salad which combined the herring fillets with a mixture of chopped shallots, gherkins, apples and that characteristic Scandinavian herb, dill, bound with soured cream. Another recipe is for a fairly simple grilled fish, but which has some clear additional flavours.

Herring dishes should be served in true Scandinavian fashion, with plain boiled potatoes. These always formed part of the *smörgåsbord* buffet, and are a good foil to the richness of the herrings. Another potato dish which is uniquely Swedish, and formed part of the daily buffet at the Grand, was Jansson's *Frestelse* or Temptation. It was apparently named after a certain gentleman whose religious principles forbade eating for pleasure, but who was sorely tempted by this dish, a combination of potatoes, anchovies and cream!

The cold kitchen in the Grand was staffed entirely by

Matjes Herring in Apple and Dill Soured Cream Dressing

SERVES 4

6 fresh *matjes* herring fillets	Cut into fine strips about 1.5 cm (¾ in) wide. Place in a serving dish.
½ eating apple, peeled and cut into segments **2 small pickled gherkins, sliced** **2 shallots, peeled and sliced**	Add to the herring fillets.
1 small pot soured cream **15 ml (1 tablespoon) cotton tofu** **5 ml (1 teaspoon) Dijon mustard** **juice of ½ lemon** **15 ml (1 tablespoon) finely snipped fresh dill** **salt and freshly ground pepper**	Mix together then mix carefully with the herring, apple and shallot. Season to taste, and chill for about an hour.
1 small cooked beetroot, cut into thin slices **15 ml (1 tablespoon) vinaigrette** **a pinch of sugar**	Marinate together for at least 15 minutes. To serve, place a circle of beetroot slices on the plates, and then arrange the herring salad on top.
250 g (9 oz) new potatoes, scrubbed and boiled	Serve hot with the salad.

women, which I have since discovered is fairly traditional in Scandinavia. It seemed very unusual to me, because the profession tends to be male dominated in almost every other country. It was the first time I had worked with so many women, and I enjoyed myself thoroughly. I have subsequently worked a great deal with women, >

The Grand Hotel in Stockholm, as it was in 1975. I chose to work here because of the herrings!

Grilled Herrings with Fennel

SERVES 4   OVEN: Moderate, 180°C/350°F/Gas 4

4 herrings, each about 200 g (7 oz), gutted 85 ml (3 fl oz) light olive oil	Marinate together for about an hour, turning over occasionally. Remove the herrings from the oil and pour the oil into an ovenproof dish.
salt and freshly ground pepper	Season the fish and place under a hot grill for about 1 minute on each side.
1 bay leaf 8 sprigs fennel	Add to the olive oil in the dish. Place the herrings on top, baste with oil and bake in the preheated oven for about 5 minutes.
4 sprigs parsley 2 lemons, halved	Serve the fish garnished with the fennel, parsley and lemon halves, and sprinkled with a little of the olive oil.

Jansson's Temptation

SERVES 4   OVEN: Hot, 220°C/425°F/Gas 7

25 g (1 oz) butter	Use a little to grease a large casserole.
675 g (1½ lb) potatoes, peeled and cut into strips	Arrange half in the buttered dish.
2 large onions, peeled and sliced into rings	Arrange half on top of the potatoes.
6 Swedish anchovies, filleted and sliced, or 12 pieces anchovies in oil	Arrange on top of the onions, then cover with the remaining onion then the remaining potato. Season the layers with pepper and a very little salt. Drizzle over a little liquid or oil from the cans if liked. Put pieces of the remaining butter on top.
200 ml (7 fl oz) whipping cream	Pour half into the casserole over the contents, and transfer to the preheated oven. Bake for 20 minutes or until the potatoes are golden, then reduce the oven temperature to 190°/375°F/Gas 5. Pour in the remaining cream and bake until the potatoes are tender, about another 20–30 minutes.

ANTON'S TIP

The anchovies canned in Sweden are actually smelts or sprats; they are pickled with spices, and come whole or in skinned or boned fillets

Marinated Trout Fillets with Dill Yoghurt Sauce

SERVES 4

5 ml (1 teaspoon) sea salt 15 ml (1 tablespoon) caster sugar 10 ml (2 teaspoons) coarsely ground pepper juice of 1 orange and 1 lemon 1 bunch fresh dill	For the marinade, mix together. Place half of the mixture in a tray just large enough to hold the fish fillets.
8 river trout fillets, skinned and trimmed, bones removed with tweezers	Place in the tray, and sprinkle the rest of the marinade on top. Cover with foil and press, using some weights. Leave to marinate in a cool place for at least 4 hours. Remove the fish from the marinade. Quickly rinse the fish in cold water, and pat dry.
150 g (5 oz) natural yoghurt 2 tomatoes, skinned, seeded and finely diced 30 ml (2 tablespoons) finely snipped dill lemon juice salt and freshly ground pepper	Stir together, and season to taste. Serve this sauce with the trout fillets.

Paper-Thin Salmon with Lime and Chervil

SERVES 4

350 g (12 oz) fresh fillet of salmon	Cut into paper-thin slices.
juice of 2 limes 50 g (2 fl oz) olive oil salt and freshly ground pepper	Mix the lime juice with the olive oil, then lightly brush over the centre of four plates. Season with salt and pepper. Arrange the salmon slices on the plates and brush with more oil and lime juice.
20 ml (4 teaspoons) salmon caviar (Keta) grated zest of 1 lime, blanched a few chervil leaves	Use to garnish the salmon.

ANTON'S TIP

It goes without saying that the fish has to be very fresh for this dish.

   Another good garnish addition is cracked red peppercorns – about 10 ml (2 teaspoons).

and make a point of employing them in my kitchen. Indeed, until very recently, my principal assistant has been a woman, Kit Chan. (She has moved on, to Australia as Head Chef at the new Observatory Hotel in Sydney.)

   Another dish I learned to prepare while working at the Grand was *gravadlax*, the famous Scandinavian marinated salmon (although other fish are prepared in similar ways as well). The fish is not cooked at all, but marinated for a couple of days with salt, sugar and various flavour-

ings, primarily dill – often with a dash of the local spirit, *akvavit*, as well. The fish is weighted and turned, and when cut, usually more thickly than smoked salmon, the flesh is buttery rich, and full of flavour. I still do this in the traditional way with salmon, but the basic idea works well with trout as well, as in the above recipe.

   With fish as fresh as that in Scandinavia, it can be eaten virtually raw as they do in Japan. Having learned the principles in Sweden, I often marinate thin slices of salmon simply in some lemon or lime juice and other flavourings. >

(Do the same with turbot or trout.)

Perhaps the next most important influence of that brief three-month stay in Sweden was the plate service. The section in which I worked also prepared banquets – often for up to 400 people, and the individual servings were all pre-plated in the kitchen. Up until then, my experience had been of silver service, a waiter serving foods from a platter directly to the diners at the table. Pre-plating at home in Switzerland was associated in my mind with quick, less expensive foods, but this new idea suddenly seemed much more efficient and attractive, and it was to change my thinking very considerably.

From Sweden I arranged to spend the next few months at the famous Villa Lorraine restaurant in Brussels. At that time it was the only restaurant outside France to have been given three stars by the *Guide Michelin* and with that kind of accolade I just had to see what it was like and what made it so special. Its reputation for serving the very finest food, I soon discovered, was fully justified. I helped out on various sections, almost like a trainee, because this wasn't so much a job as an opportunity to see how the kitchen operated.

It was very serious food indeed. The chef, Camille Lurkin, held a cigar permanently in his mouth. He was a wonderful man and ran an excellent team, though sadly he was to die when still relatively young. I had first met him when he came to St Moritz to head a food promotion at the Kulm Hotel. I was very impressed by the man himself and by his style of cooking. I remember watching him prepare a rack of lamb with a very plain sauce. When I asked if that were to be all, did he not want to add anything else, he said no. The best food is the simplest food, the plainer the better, he claimed, and I've kept that in mind ever since.

The standards Monsieur Lurkin demanded in his kitchen were exceptionally high. Everything was cooked freshly, à *la minute*. There was no question of dishes or sauces simply being reheated when the orders came downstairs. There was no cheating here. The stocks and sauces had to be properly reduced and to prove it there wasn't a bag of flour outside the pastry section!

The style of cooking was very classical, but there were already touches of the modern. I was very impressed. The restaurant was expensive, serving a lot of people from the embassies, and the service too was very professional. The recipe that most reminds me of the Villa Lorraine uses crayfish. Huge tanks at the restaurant held shoals of these freshwater crustacea and we sold hundreds every day. The recipe is fiddly, admittedly, but it looks good and tastes spectacular.

I loved Brussels, it's a beautiful city, and I loved the mentality of the people. It's also very much a food city, with high quality demanded even of its street food – mussels and *frites*! I lived fairly near to the Villa Lorraine with a family and walked to work every day, enjoying every minute of the atmosphere. >

Crayfish Villa Lorraine

SERVES 4

ANTON'S TIP

This is an adaptation of the famous crayfish Villa Lorraine recipe, which uses no cream.

24 crayfish **2 litres (3½ pints) Fish Stock (see page 156)**	Place together in a large pot, bring to the boil, and cook for 2 minutes. Remove the crayfish from the stock, and start to boil 500 ml (17 fl oz) of it to reduce by half. Meanwhile, when cool enough to handle, snap the head from each crayfish and clean it out. Reserve. Peel the shell from the tails, and keep flesh warm. Discard the tail shells, claws and legs (or freeze to contribute flavour to another fish stock).
200 g (7 oz) white of leek, diced **100 g (4 oz) each of celeriac and carrots, peeled and diced** **salt and freshly ground pepper**	Add to the reduced stock and bring to the boil. Season well. Using a slotted spoon, place a little of the diced vegetable mixture into each crayfish head. Place the tail flesh on top. Divide the remaining vegetable dice and juices between four plates, and place the crayfish on top.
sprigs of fresh dill	Use to garnish, and serve immediately.

**Pierre in a moment of fun in
the kitchen at the Villa
Lorraine, Brussels.**

I worked with someone at the Villa Lorraine who has since become a very good friend. Freddy von Casserie was a *sous-chef* there under Camille Lurkin, and he has since become chef. It was Freddy who suggested I should move on to another famous Brussels restaurant, L'Ecailler du Palais Royal, which specialised in fish. This was owned by Monsieur Kreusch, a very distinguished restaurateur, well-known in the industry worldwide, who also owned the Villa Lorraine. The style of L'Ecailler had apparently been inspired by visits he had made to London, and

restaurants such as Bentley's and Wheeler's.

The chef, Robert de Koninck, insisted on only the freshest produce and there was no skimping on the butter and cream. The fish, of whatever kind, was cooked simply and presented attractively, again plated as in Stockholm. The restaurant served hundreds of oysters, some raw, some lightly cooked, and it was there that my ideas for the following recipe originated.

I had really financed these visits to Sweden and Belgium myself. Although I had been given a room to sleep in, the point in my going had been not to earn, but to learn. And learn I had, from the secrets of the herring to the basics of plate service. The entire time I was in northern Europe I was dominated by the job that was still to come – that at the Dorchester – and I was constantly working out how I could incorporate some of these new ideas into my plans for London.

I had encountered the classical tradition as interpreted in Sweden and Belgium, but it was a tradition tempered by *national* influences. I had great fun analysing how to retain the essential purity of the recipes while adapting them to my own style and tastes, and to those of the Londoners I was soon to cook for.

Poached Oysters

SERVES 4

28 oysters	Carefully open with an oyster knife or small strong knife, keeping the juices.
125 ml (4½ fl oz) Fish Stock (see page 156)	Mix with the juices. Remove the oysters from their shells and place in a pan with the stock.
juice of ½ lemon	Add to the pan, bring to the boil, and poach the oysters for 15 seconds. Remove the oysters and keep warm. Reduce the stock by half by rapid boiling.
6 oz (175 g) tomatoes, skinned, seeded and diced 2 medium courgettes, trimmed and cut into fine *julienne* strips salt and freshly ground pepper	Cook in the stock for 1 minute, then strain well and season to taste with salt and pepper. Place the oysters on serving plates – or back in their shells – and top with the tomato and courgette mixture and a little stock.
8 basil leaves	Shred very finely and use as a garnish.

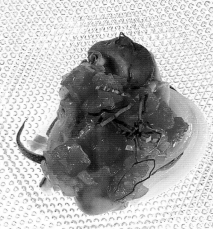

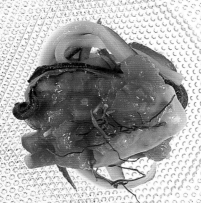
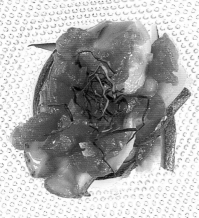

Chapter Seven

The Dorchester

I WALKED OFF THE PLANE AT HEATHROW ON JUNE 14TH 1975, CARRYING JUST ONE SUIT-
CASE OF CLOTHES AND MY PRECIOUS BOX OF KNIVES. I WAS TRAVELLING ALONE AS
KATHRIN, MY WIFE, HAD STAYED BEHIND IN SWITZERLAND TO PACK UP THE HOUSE
BEFORE JOINING ME IN LONDON ABOUT THREE MONTHS LATER. (SHE HAD ALSO JUST GIVEN
BIRTH TO OUR FIRST SON, PHILIPP. MARK WAS TO BE BORN TWO YEARS LATER IN LON-
DON.) UNTIL MY SMALL FAMILY ARRIVED, I WOULD BE STAYING IN A ROOM AT THE HOTEL.
I SLEPT FITFULLY THAT NIGHT, WONDERING, WITH A MIXTURE OF EXCITEMENT AND NOT A
LITTLE APPREHENSION, WHAT THE NEXT DAY WOULD BRING.

COMING FROM THE CONTINENT, I WAS MORE THAN AWARE OF ALL THE JOKES THAT
WERE MADE AT THE EXPENSE OF BRITISH COOKING, BUT I WAS DETERMINED NOT TO BE
BIASED. I ARRIVED, I HOPED, WITH AN OPEN MIND. THE DORCHESTER WAS FAMOUS AND
RESPECTED, AND THE TWO RESTAURANTS, THE GRILL ROOM AND THE TERRACE, WERE
POPULAR. WITH 132 CHEFS, IT WAS ONE OF THE LARGEST BRIGADES IN EUROPE. BUT THINGS
DID NOT GET OFF TO THE BEST OF STARTS. ON MY VERY FIRST DAY IT BECAME FAIRLY OBVI-
OUS THAT A LOT OF THE STAFF RESENTED MY APPOINTMENT. THEY HAD ALREADY SEEN TWO
OTHER EXECUTIVE *SOUS-CHEFS* COME AND GO. THE LAST ONE HAD ALSO BEEN SWISS, SO
WHEN I APPEARED, ANOTHER SWISS, BUT YOUNGER, THE REGULARS WERE NOT IMPRESSED.

**The Dorchester, where I
was to spend twelve happy
years and enjoy my first
experience of British
cooking.**

Rather than wait to discover whether I could cook or not, they had made up their minds before I arrived. 'I was here before he was born, what does he know at twenty-eight?' they demanded, and the longer they had been there the more aggrieved they felt.

There were six *sous-chefs* in all, and the eldest would have been around sixty whilst the youngest was easily a year older than I was. But since there was nothing I could do about that, I resolved to just sit it out. There was no point in being angry or upset. One, a Welshman who could have been little more than five foot tall and must have weighed nearly seventeen stone, came up to me that first morning. 'Good morning, chef,' he said. We spoke a few words and then he added pointedly, 'By the way, I just thought I'd let you know I have a son who is the same age as you.'

He didn't need to say any more, I got the message loud and clear.

However I was determined not to be put off on my first day, so I continued walking around the kitchen as though nothing had happened and made sure I said hello to everyone. This is something I still do now. By starting off the working day with a few words to everyone, I can judge whether they are happy or not. If someone averts their gaze, and is anxious about looking me straight in the eye, I know there is something wrong. If there is anything I can do to help, I will do it, for without good relations and happy people in the kitchen, it is impossible to achieve the best.

That first morning, I was also getting the feel of the actual cooking. At the stove I noticed the *chef potager* stirring a heavy white roux. When I asked him what he was doing he answered bluntly, 'Tomato soup, of course. Only I forgot to put the tomato in it.' With that, he opened a tin of tomato purée.

I was stunned. Was that really the way they prepared the soups? I said nothing more, there would be time

enough for that. But, a little further on, I was stopped short by the extraordinary sight of a wooden ladle standing upright in a pot of sauce.

'Don't you think this sauce is a bit thick?' I said to the *chef saucier*.

'Oh no, chef,' he replied. 'I haven't had a single complaint in my twenty-five years as *chef saucier*.'

I don't think any of those chefs were aware of the revolution in food that was taking place around the world. If they *were* aware of it they probably dismissed it as foreign nonsense. Like most of my peers I believed strongly that food should be as fresh and lightly cooked as possible and that sauces, far from being a heavy porridge of flour, must be reduced from the cooking juices to which a little cream or butter was added. Never mind the rest of the world, here they remained deeply suspicious of change.

After a couple of months, I still had not made much headway, but I felt I had to persevere. My wife and baby son were just about to leave Switzerland, and the furniture and luggage were already in transit.

So that was that, there was no turning back now, and I resigned myself to a tough few months ahead. Thankfully, Mr Käufeler and I got on well which reassured me a good deal, and at least we were able to work together closely without any friction.

But when I talked to any of the 132 chefs it was only too apparent that the main reason most of them were doing the job was only to earn a living, and generally they spent the working day longing for the moment when they could leave. To me that seemed a great shame. Cooking is a skill and a vocation, and I really believe you should only enter the profession if you are prepared to work hard and be truly dedicated to producing your best. With no love, there is no point in embarking on an apprenticeship because it is not the kind of job you can do half-heartedly.

It was hardly surprising then that the quality of the food suffered. There was nothing wrong with the basic ingredients, nothing at least that some judicial buying couldn't put right. Britain produces some of the very finest foods – wonderful seafood and the best beef and lamb – but all too often, simply as a result of uncaring buyers, the fruit would be under-ripe when it came into the kitchen or the fish not that fresh. These, however, were all problems that I knew could be solved without much difficulty.

The real trouble lay with the way the food was then treated. It is vital that food is handled carefully or it will spoil, and for the very best results, it must then be prepared sensitively and cooked with love. Instead the chefs tended to stick to the old ways, drowning delicate flavours with strong-tasting sauces and gravies. It was going to be hard, I realised, to change their habits but gradually, by cooking dishes for them and showing them how I wanted a sauce to look, I was able to bring my influence to bear.

Often I would talk through a recipe with the chefs, discussing the methods, ingredients and the 'chemistry' of cooking. Why, I would ask, does milk boil over when a pot of water doesn't? Why does a soufflé rise? Slowly, with time, plenty of encouragement and demonstrations, I began to win their confidence.

Another problem concerned taste. The widespread dependence on pre-cooked and packaged food had also done much to destroy most of the national palate. Once customers get used to indifferent food, they become complacent. Whereas on the Continent a badly cooked dish would be sent straight back to the kitchen, in Britain people seemed less inclined to complain. It was a long road I had to travel, but as time moved on and I began to feel I was making some impression, I was able to realistically entertain the idea of one day achieving something here of which I could be proud.

Certainly my major concern was the chefs. They were a varied bunch, and they included some extraordinary characters. There was one hippy, who tucked his long hair up under his chef's hat, and who often came into work looking as though he had been high the whole night, which no doubt he had! Then there was a very small man with short cropped hair, a real London lad. He used to stalk round the kitchen looking for trouble and whenever you saw him outside work, at a party say, he always turned up with a gang of henchmen, all of whom were shorter than he was. He was quick to start a fight, and I always suspected that he was up to no good, although he was nice and willing in the kitchen. So it came as no surprise to learn, years later, that he ended up inside. The story, I heard, was that he had been involved in a robbery at a building society. He had been sitting in the getaway car outside, waiting for his mates. Whilst he sat there revving the engine, his accomplices slipped out of a side door and drove off in another car, leaving him to face the music!

There was also an oddball apprentice who, on being asked to fetch a cheese from the larder, proceeded to carve the Cheddar into a pyramid. When the *chef garde-manger* saw this apparition he demanded to know precisely what the apprentice thought he was doing.

'But chef,' pleaded the innocent fool, 'the order was for a sharp cheese and I can't get it any sharper.'

More seriously though, I was very shocked to overhear one of the *sous-chefs*, a man who had worked in the kitchen for over twenty-five years, answer the phone and then shout out through the internal tunnel speaker: 'Anyone here called Jack Smith?' I couldn't believe my ears. Maybe that doesn't strike you as that strange, but I promise that in all my experience of working in kitchens, I had never come across a chef with that lack of interest in his colleagues. I was used to everyone sharing their lives, and knowing not just the chefs' names, but their wives', girlfriends' and children's names too.

If that came as a shock, there were plenty of other surprises in store. At lunchtime one of the *commis de rang* came down from the Grill Room and told the *sous-chef* on duty that he needed a minute steak. The >

The Grill Room at the Dorchester, in which we served the best of British ingredients and dishes.

Matelote d'Anguille

SERVES 4

1 kg (2¼ lb) fresh eels, skinned and filleted salt and freshly ground pepper	Cut into pieces 5–6 cm (2–2¼ in) long. Season with salt and pepper.
75 g (3 oz) button mushrooms, stalks chopped 25 g (1 oz) leek, finely chopped 25 g (1 oz) carrot, finely chopped 2 shallots, peeled and finely chopped 1 garlic clove, peeled and crushed 1 bouquet garni 350 ml (12 fl oz) red wine	Reserve mushroom caps whole, and place all remaining ingredients in a pan. Boil and reduce by one-third.
200 ml (7 fl oz) Fish Stock (see page 156)	Add, simmer for 30 minutes to reduce by a third. Strain.
12 button onions, peeled 90 g (3½ oz) butter	Cook in 50 g (2 oz) of the butter for 15 minutes until tender. Add the mushroom caps for the last few minutes. Keep warm. Add remaining butter to the pan, then cook the eel gently until tender, but not coloured.
15 ml (1 tablespoon) *beurre manié* (see Tip) 10 ml (2 teaspoons) tomato paste (optional)	Bring the sauce to the boil, whisk in the *beurre manié* and the tomato paste (if using) to enhance the colour. Then check seasoning. Place the eel in a warmed dish, and cover with the mushrooms, onion and sauce.
30 ml (2 tablespoons) finely chopped parsley	Sprinkle over the eel in the dish or on individual plates and serve piping hot.

ANTON'S TIP

For *beurre manié* to thicken the sauce, mix together equal amounts of butter and plain flour.

Serve croûtons with the *matelote* if liked (see page 52).

sous-chef passed the message on to the *garde-manger* through the tunnel speaker but nothing happened. And this while I could clearly see five chefs, including a *chef de partie*, standing around chatting at the nearby roast section. As the minutes ticked by, not one of them responded to the order.

It wasn't that they hadn't heard the order, their problem was one of attitude. 'That's not my job,' they used to say when asked to do something beyond their job description. To cut a long story short, after several more vain requests, the Grill Room manager himself had to come down. Seething with fury, the *sous-chef* stormed the twenty yards over to the refrigerator, returned with the steak on a plate and virtually threw it at the *chef de partie*, with a few choice words.

Phew! What an effort just for one steak. It made me exhausted just thinking about the time and energy wasted through sheer bloody-mindedness. There wasn't a thought of putting the customer first, and rather than seeing themselves as part of a team striving to achieve the best for their restaurant or reputation, these chefs just saw themselves as individuals, out to get what they could from the system and determined not to be put upon or ill-used. It was extremely dispiriting.

In fact I considered many of the chefs did extremely well for themselves, sometimes working far fewer hours than their counterparts on the Continent. Imagine, they actually had an arrangement whereby everyone working in the *garde-manger* was allowed home at three in the afternoon if all the dishes had been prepared for that evening. This meant that they worked maybe six or >

IT IS VITAL THAT FOOD IS HANDLED CAREFULLY OR IT WILL BE SPOILED, AND FOR TH

seven hours a day with 1½ hours off for meal breaks! As for the dishes, the quality suffered after sitting in the warming cupboard for a long time.

Then there were the staff lunch breaks. To my astonishment the *chefs de partie* and first *commis* took an hour off for lunch between two and three o'clock, when the restaurant was still very busy, leaving the kitchen to be run by the *sous-chefs* with only some of the *commis* and apprentices to help them. And those lunches! Rather than having a staff cook, the chefs were allowed to select whatever they liked from the restaurant menu. Lobster Thermidor and fillet steak went down a treat followed by fresh strawberries or whatever they fancied from the range of desserts. It was quite incredible. If several chefs ordered the same thing, say a steak and

My predecessor at the Dorchester, Eugène Käufeler, when he retired at the age of sixty-eight.

kidney pudding, it could well mean that the customer who ordered a portion of pudding at quarter-past two would have to go without!

In those first months, it was hard to keep my counsel, but I had to content myself with observing and making mental notes of the changes I would like to make when I became head chef.

On December 15th that same year, I took over as *Chef des Cuisines*. Eugène Käufeler became Executive Chef and the new arrangement not only gave me a larger say in the day-to-day running of the kitchen, but also, and far more important to me, a great deal of encouragement to start putting into practice some of my ideas.

I think it was probably at that point that the split in loyalties became apparent. Some of the older chefs were against any changes. The younger ones, who were more open to new ideas, enjoyed working with me. Many carried on working with me for a few years, before going on to make their own names elsewhere. Among them were Michael Bonacini who was chef at the Windsor Arms, Toronto, John Hornsby, formerly the chef at Harrods, and Philip Britten, *Chef de Cuisine* at London's Capital Hotel.

John Hornsby told me recently how he remembered me saying that service was like a set of traffic lights. On red, you're still, on amber you get ready and green was for go. At the time he was so drilled in the hot-plate mentality, that he didn't have a clue what I was talking about. But he certainly does now!

As well as introducing the idea of cooking the food at the very last moment, I was determined to try and standardise the dishes. There were three working shifts in the kitchen and ever since I had joined, I had been bothered by the fact that although they followed the same recipes, the results were always different. So I asked the chefs to bring me samples each day of what they prepared so that we could bring them all to the same standard.

The *chef potager* at the time was one of the stalwarts of the kitchen and a law unto himself. Every day he brought the soups in on a tray for me to taste. There would have been about twelve soups in all in little cups, an idea picked up years before from Henri Dessibourg.

BEST RESULTS IT MUST THEN BE PREPARED SENSITIVELY AND COOKED WITH LOVE.

Some needed more seasoning, others more cream, and each day there was always some adjustment to make. Then one day he arrived as usual with the tray of soups and this time, at last, they had worked. The *chef potager* left, clearly delighted.

A few minutes later I left the office too and discovered him wrapping the cups in cling film.

'What are you doing?' I asked.

'Oh, it's you,' he said, 'I thought if you liked them that much you could have them again tomorrow! Save me a lot of trouble, wouldn't it?'

Pity for him that it wasn't that easy trying to fool me!

This wasn't the only chef who would try to play clever. There was another whose favourite trick was to claim he was short-staffed for banquets. He would ask each *chef de partie* in turn whether they would be able to spare an extra hand.

'Have you seen the function sheet?' he would say. 'I'm stuck with no staff. What am I going to do?'

By the time he'd gone round the whole kitchen, he had amassed enough staff for him to be able to sit with nothing to do but give out instructions to the others whilst he sat drinking coffee.

Keen to engage the chefs' interest in their work, I started to enter the brigade for cookery competitions. This I thought would be an excellent way of inspiring them to create finer dishes and to bring in a spirit of competitiveness. I am convinced healthy competition is a great motivator.

In August 1976 we won five gold medals and a major award at the Berne Exhibition in Switzerland, and the following year I selected four chefs to come with me to Germany for another exhibition in Frankfurt. One was Alan Hill, now at the famous Scottish hotel, Gleneagles. Another of the chosen was Nobby Clark, by now well over 60, the *sous-chef* who had been sensitive about my age. After what he had said to me, no-one could understand why I had picked him, but a good deal of time had passed and over the months he had become a friend.

Those exhibitions were tough and after twenty-four hours working non-stop, we produced a total of forty-five different dishes. Once again we were awarded five gold medals and a major gold award, and I shall never forget the moment when we heard those results. Overcome by the fact that he had won a gold medal, Nobby burst into tears. He was so pleased that he couldn't stop grinning for the rest of the day, and I noticed that he wore the medal on the way back in the plane. It was wonderful to see that he had gained so much pleasure from cooking, and I was told that whenever he went into the pub after work he proudly wore his medal.

Other chefs who came with me to these exhibitions from the Dorchester over the years included Ray Neve, now my head chef at Mosimann's, and Colin Ryall, who is an experimental chef for Marks & Spencer.

With the following year came the first of what were to be a succession of changes in management. A new managing director, Peter Stafford, was appointed and with so much in a state of flux, Eugène Käufeler decided this was an appropriate time for him to retire. And thus it was that on November 1st 1976 I became the *Maître Chef des Cuisines* at the Dorchester.

I took over responsibility for the Grill Room and the Terrace, for our twenty-four-hour room service, and for the Dorchester banquets, frequently for up to 1,000 people. There was one large kitchen in those days with only pastry and bakery as separate kitchens. The Grill Room served mainly British food – grills, roasts etc – and the Terrace was more international in concept. I had ideas of what I wanted to change in both, and over the next few months Peter Stafford and I had many discussions as we got to know each other's tastes, ambitions and needs, and very quickly became friends.

I also wanted to make some changes in the kitchen staff, but I have never believed in just sacking people. Instead, I preferred to focus on the good points in individuals, and to start by working with those. I think success is far more likely if one starts by taking a positive approach and consequently, though I was keen to replace about eight or nine of the positions, I did this by creating new positions so that I could re-motivate people, and make them take up new challenges.

For one thing it had always seemed to me ridiculous that the chef in charge of the fish section never ate seafood himself, and when he went abroad on holiday, he actually took with him enough prepared sandwiches to last several days because he didn't like foreign food!

Thankfully he later took over responsibility for the night shift, enabling a fish and seafood lover to take on this central role.

Keen to find a new *chef rôtisseur*, I asked Ernie, the chef who had been in charge of roasting, to take over the new position of bottling preserved fruits. Peter Stafford was keen that we should serve fresh fruits all year round, and each year, for instance, we produced up to 10,000 bottled peaches. It was a job that Ernie did with great pride. Subsequently I asked him if he would take on the important position of looking after cost control and the kitchen audit, including the administration of the pay roll. We were then able to train a young and keen kitchen porter to bottle the peaches which was a good step up for him whilst Ernie proved to be an excellent auditor. I came to trust him completely and was able to sign the papers on Monday morning without really having to check them. In fact he was so good, so precise and well organised that his talents had not been used to the full in the kitchen.

In another case I wanted to have a new *chef saucier*. The present chef had been in the job for over twenty-five years, and I felt it was time for a fresh approach. I wanted him to take over as breakfast chef which can be an unpopular position. It's a bit of a backwater for a young chef at the start of his career, since it involves coming in very early in the morning and leaving before the real action starts. However, for this man it seemed the ideal solution. He was loyal , a quality still to be valued, but he was also very proud. I knew that I was going to have to work hard to sell him the idea as exciting and positive.

'If you came in early in the morning,' I told him, 'you would then be able to go home early as well and spend the rest of the day with your family, watch TV, work in the garden . . .'

It took a lot of encouragement on my part, but eventually he realised that there was a lot of sense in what I was saying. Finally one morning, several weeks later, he came into my office and announced that he thought he would like to take over the breakfasts so that he could spend more time at home.

In no way had I forced him to take this decision. It was one that he had come to himself, and consequently it worked very well. He was very happy coming in early and I was delighted to be able to bring in an excellent new and enthusiastic *chef saucier*. Two very important positions were filled, two men were happy, and the kitchen worked more efficiently.

Six months later, when the chefs realised I was not going to give everyone their notice, all but seven decided to leave the union. That was a real sign that we were progressing. I had also had much support from my older *sous-chefs*, including Roy, Maurice and Brian.

I consider that I was extremely fortunate in having Peter Stafford as my first managing director. He was a marvellous man to work with. Firstly, he had plenty of experience, having spent six years as managing director at the Hotel Mandarin in Hong Kong, and prior to that sixteen at the Savoy. He also gave me all the support I needed, particularly vital at the beginning, when there were so many radical changes to make in the hotel in general, not just in the kitchen. He was a true professional, a hard and firm manager because he knew what he wanted and usually got it, a quality I greatly admired. To me he was like a father, tough but always supportive, and he also loved his food, which of course meant a great deal to me. Surrounded by a prevailing attitude of apathy, it was marvellous to have the vigorous backing of someone who really understood what I was trying to do in the kitchen.

One of the first decisions we made together was to build a new kitchen next to the Grill Room. Like myself, Peter believed that food which is cooked should not have to travel too far, and that it should preferably be prepared and cooked as close as possible to the restaurant. I was really grateful for Peter's support and the decision was a true breakthrough. The whole food concept of the Grill Room changed dramatically from that day onwards.

But there seemed to me to be so many other glaring anomalies that had built up over the years, and I was determined to resolve them. Another initial decision I made as *Maître Chef des Cuisines* was to start each day with a meeting of senior staff at which we discussed all the functions, the birthday parties and cakes, *à la carte* dishes, and any banquets or buffets. The idea behind this decision was to instill some mutual trust and respect amongst the staff. I was determined to put an end to the divisiveness, this 'us and them' mentality.

Soon it became possible to tackle some practical issues. First of all, I wanted to reduce the number of items on the three menus. At that time there were over a hundred different dishes offered and obviously it was almost impossible for the brigade to prepare that many each day and only use fresh ingredients.

Next I decided to tackle some of the problems in the banqueting service, and put some of the ideas I'd encountered in Canada and Sweden into practice. Up

until then, the cold first courses had been prepared in services of ten and the poor waiter had to divide the dish into ten equal parts at the table. This of course was difficult for him to judge and more often than not the first person served would be presented with a beautiful slice of terrine whilst the last person usually got the small tail end. Moreover, as each helping was served, the remainder on the dish looked less and less appetising.

From my previous experience in banqueting, I knew it would be far nicer for each dish to be prepared in the kitchen where there was more time to ensure that every plate was individually dressed. This meant of course that the chefs would have to stay on in the kitchen, rather than dashing off home as soon as they had prepared the food. Originally there was a good deal of grumbling but once they saw what I was doing and realised what a difference it made, they soon came round.

One of the most popular main courses for these large functions was roast saddle of lamb which we often prepared for as many as 800 guests. Whichever way you look at it, this is obviously a fairly mammoth

task, but never had I seen it done in quite such a complicated and ill-judged fashion. On the day of the banquet the *chef rôtisseur* came in at four o'clock in the morning to roast all the saddles of lamb. He let them cool off before slicing the meat and putting it back on the bone. The saddles were then reheated in the hotplate and served at eight or nine o'clock in the evening. Naturally this system was capable of producing only one result – very unhappy meat.

Step by step, I altered all this. Meat should only be handled raw, minimally once cooked, and it should be served straightaway. The very first change I made to that banqueting menu was to replace the roast by a stuffed saddle of lamb, which was roasted and carved at the last minute. This was a great success, resulting in succulent tasty lamb, even though there was more last-minute work. British lamb, especially Welsh lamb, is a great favourite of mine, and the recipe overleaf is how I most like to serve it now.

From changing menus to training the chefs, I had my work cut out. In order to help the chefs understand what it was I wanted from them I had started holding weekly training sessions which they were all encour-

I have always been passionate about cars. My springer spaniel, Tommy, enjoys them too. This 1936 Vauxhall gave me a lot of happy hours.

aged to attend. During these sessions I went back over the basics of good cooking. I talked about steaming, grilling and poaching, skills you might think they already had, but the difference was in the approach. Rather than boiling broccoli until it was limp, I wanted to show how much better the vegetable was if steamed over a light stock and removed when just *al dente*. It then kept its brilliant colour and all its flavour. And I wanted to demonstrate how a fillet of turbot that was poached in a little well seasoned *court bouillon* and then left to cool in the juices remained firm, yet moist, and tasted so good on its own served warm. It no longer needed to be drowned in a rich butter sauce.

At first there was some scepticism, but in time these sessions became a major attraction for young chefs who were starting out on their careers.

It is a matter of great pride to me that many exciting and adventurous young chefs now in hotels and restaurants all over the world had spent some time with me, and that I perhaps exerted some small influence upon them. I've been privileged to work with them and to be friends with them. They include Idris Caldora (Churchill, London), David Cavalier (a Michelin-starred chef, now at L'Escargot in London), Michael Coaker (Mayfair, London), Iain Donald (SAS, Manchester), Anton Edelman (Savoy, London), Robert Elsmore (Hunstrete House Hotel, Bristol), Alan Ford (Hintlesham Hall, Ipswich), Stephen Goodlad (Burnham Beeches Country House, Victoria, Australia), Michael Hicks (Caprice, London), Clive Howe (Lygon Arms, Broadway), Marcus Moore (Royal Garden Hotel, Hong Kong), Tony Osborne (pastry chef at the Hong Kong Hilton), Paul Reed (Chester Grosvenor), John Webber (Kinnaird House, Perthshire), Hans-Ulrich Wismer (Westin Chosun Beach in Korea), and many more.

Whilst I was doing my best to try and change attitudes, there were some of the old school whom I knew would never really change. Gradually though, as my >

Tenderloin of Welsh Lamb with Herbs and Grain Mustard

SERVES 4

4 × 120g (4½ oz) noisettes of Welsh lamb, cut from the loin	Trim well, cutting off all fat.
1 garlic clove, peeled and chopped 1 sprig thyme 1 sprig rosemary 30 ml (2 tablespoons) olive oil	Place with the lamb in a dish and marinate for at least a couple of hours.
salt and freshly ground pepper	Season the lamb and char-grill or grill for 2–3 minutes on each side, leaving it pink.
10 ml (2 teaspoons) each of Dijon and grain mustard	Mix together and use to brush over one side of each piece of lamb.
60 ml (4 tablespoons) finely cut chives (or a mixture of parsley, chives, basil, tarragon)	Place in a plate and dip the mustard-coated side of the lamb noisettes in it. Shake off any surplus.
about 200 ml (7 fl oz) Brown Lamb Stock (see page 157), reduced by half 5 ml (1 teaspoon) grain mustard	Heat together.
225 g (8 oz) peeled sliced vegetables (carrots, red onions, baby leeks), steamed or stir-fried in a little butter	Season well, then divide between four plates, coat with a little of the sauce, and serve the lamb on top.

With the late Danny Kaye, who was not only one of my best friends, but also was a very good cook, especially of Chinese food. Danny and I spent many many happy moments together.

influence took hold, the more difficult types left of their own accord.

I still had a few challenges. Though I never tried to stop anyone drinking, except when it interfered with work, I seemed to have a moderating effect. When I became Executive Chef the end of shift orders for drinks were usually in the ratio of eighty beers to twenty mineral waters. A year later, I'm pleased to say, the order had been revised to about ten beers and ninety mineral waters!

Inevitably, too, there was the occasional girl trouble. I remember one day an American film crew came round the kitchen to make a documentary. Amongst the crew were some attractive girls who were arousing a good deal of interest from the chefs. Thinking no more of it, I left the hotel that night and returned the following morning to discover a report on my desk. Two of the chefs had not checked out their cards the night before and it transpired that they had spent the night at the hotel. The management immediately called for their dismissal and I had to fight quite hard to keep their jobs, because they were good lads, and had great talent. (I won't give *their* names!) In fact this was a very rare incident and certainly never interfered with the running of the kitchen.

A more serious problem as far as I was concerned, however, was the fact that for the last twenty-five years it had been traditional for all the first *commis* to take Sunday off, despite the fact that half the kitchen staff were off for the weekend, which already left the kitchen very short of hands. Realising I was treading on sacred territory, I nevertheless determined to do something to improve the weekend support.

The first *commis* were totally against the idea of working on Sundays, but gradually I managed to gently persuade them. They were able to see that it would benefit the hotel and thereby their own reputations. This willing agreement was worth waiting for because a man who *chooses* to change will keep to his word.

I was greatly relieved because I knew that this kitchen revolution was absolutely essential if I was going to be able to transform the menus. Equally vital too, was the decision to rebuild the kitchens, so streamlining operations and improving efficiency. Indeed, I was so concerned that the job should be done properly that I delayed a trip to California where we had been asked to put on a special gastronomic week at the Beverly Wilshire Hotel in Los Angeles.

So much of what I was doing then was an effort and it seems ridiculous now to think of the fuss I caused the day I first took frozen peas off the Dorchester menu and replaced them with the 'new' and 'exotic' mangetout. The head waiter was really worried.

'You can't do that,' he said. 'You have to offer people peas. Who do you think you are?'

Like others, he thought I was too determined to bring about change at any cost, but thankfully I knew I could rely on Peter Stafford to back me. In time, of course, mangetout were seen by most people as no more threatening than baby carrots, and everyone who chose those fresh, bright green and crisp flat pods from Jersey agreed with me.

Of course the quality of the produce was all important and I introduced the idea of having a special buyer who was expert at selecting the freshest vegetables or sweetest cuts of meat. From time to time, we visited all the wonderful London food markets, New Covent Garden, Billingsgate as it was then, and Smithfield. We were all impressed by the variety of produce on offer and determined to establish two cardinal rules in the kitchen: one, the produce must be as fresh as possible; and, two, it must be eaten in season. Fresh strawberries in early summer taste out of this world, but imported varieties throughout the winter are rarely as good, and can sometimes be watery and flavourless. And worse, by being able to eat them all year round, you lose the joy that comes from waiting.

It's the same with my favourite game bird, grouse. As

WHEREVER I AM, WHETHER IN LONDON OR ABROAD, I AM ALWAYS BUSY, AN

I SEARCH LOCAL MARKETS AND VISIT PEOPLE'S HOMES BECAUSE TH

My first television appearance in March, 1978, in Los Angeles, with Peter Stafford on the Dinah Shore Show.

the months and days pass waiting for the Glorious Twelfth, the excitement builds until at last you taste that first mouthful. Nothing can beat it, so why let the original delicacy be spoiled by second-class substitutes? I love roasting the birds in the traditional British way, but the grouse suprême recipe overleaf was always very popular on the Grill Room menu.

With the kitchen operating successfully, I was able to put my mind to other things, like the week in California. Although a week may seem a short time, in culinary terms the project was massive and took nearly a year in the planning. Since I always prefer to use local produce we decided to use these where available for creating our specialities. But when it came to smoked salmon and English cheeses, we chose to send these by air to California. We also had a problem with the passionfruit soufflé, one of our most popular desserts (see page 114). The trouble was that I could not find anywhere in California where we could buy fresh passionfruit, so in the end we sent the juice out by plane too!

The week was a great success and paved the way for a number of similar projects. What with these, the competitions and the publication, in 1981, of my first book, *Cuisine à la Carte*, life was certainly full.

We returned to LA in 1981 and spent two weeks touring Boston, Washington and Chicago representing the Dorchester with promotions and cookery demonstrations. In Washington we were lucky enough to be taken on a tour of the White House by the Head Chef, Henry Haller, and were very impressed by the kitchens there. Back in London again, we were invited in September to cook dinner at 10 Downing Street in honour of a state visit.

But these were awkward times to be too busy elsewhere and to be introducing change, as the Dorchester was constantly changing hands. In 1979 I had learned that Peter Stafford was leaving. This was a great blow to me personally, as I had been through so much with Peter and was very fond of him. Those first, and most

difficult, changes in the kitchen and in the menu had been made possible only by Peter's continual support.

The new manager, however, although another lover of food, was replaced three weeks later as a result of internal politics. Another lasted a year, and it wasn't until much later that I found another friend in Udo Schlentrich. He was a delightful man and an excellent manager (though he too was eventually moved on).

His was a new style of management, and he was like a fresh wind blowing through the Art Deco corridors of the Dorchester. If Peter Stafford had been like a father to me, Udo was my brother. Some of the best moments of my life have been spent in his company.

IEN I'M NOT IN THE KITCHEN I AM LOOKING FOR NEW IDEAS AND INSPIRATION.

VHERE YOU REALLY FIND THE HEART OF A COUNTRY'S CUISINE.

At the Corviglia Club in St Moritz, with Udo Schlentrich (on my left) and Hartley Mathis. We escaped for lunch and spent a few hours laughing, after which the ski-ing downhill was very easy!

One weekend, for instance, I was to cook at the Dracula Club in St Moritz. I drove out with the food and an assistant, and Udo joined us en route, bringing with him another fifty-five duck breasts in case I had been stopped at Customs. When we arrived at our destination, I wanted to go on a bobsleigh immediately. However Udo insisted, 'The food first, *then* you go down'. I think he was nervous that, if I broke my neck, *he* would have to cook the dinner!

With Udo's help, support and considerable input of ideas, between us we changed the whole concept of food at the hotel. At our first meeting, for instance, I told him of my ambition to gain two Michelin stars, and one of our first decisions made together was to revamp the Terrace restaurant, which duly came to pass.

It was to re-open in November of 1981. It had been completely redesigned and was beautifully decorated. Fourteen painters had worked for months hand-painting the pillars and arches in pink and green and picking out the details in gold leaf. The floor had also been raised three feet above the original level which meant that customers now had a view over Hyde Park from their tables. My task was to create a suitable menu.

As you may have realised by now, the appearance of food is most important to me and I wanted to create a menu that was light and elegant, especially for the restaurant. The only problem was that I felt restricted by the traditional three courses. I wanted instead to give every customer the opportunity to enjoy a far greater range of dishes. >

Suprême of Grouse with Mushrooms in a Game Sauce

SERVES 4

8 breasts of grouse salt and freshly ground pepper	Season well with salt and pepper.
80 g (3¼ oz) butter a sprig of fresh rosemary	Heat half the butter in a pan with the rosemary and brown the breasts quickly on both sides. Drain and keep to one side.
16 small onions, peeled 75 g (3 oz) lardons (small strips of bacon)	Brown in the butter remaining in the pan, and keep to one side with the grouse breasts.
175 g (6 oz) small mushrooms (button, *cèpes*, chanterelles, morels etc), cleaned	Sweat in the other half of the butter in the grouse pan for a few minutes. Return the grouse and onions to the pan.
25 ml (1 fl oz) Cognac 120 ml (4 fl oz) Madeira	Add to the pan and flame. Remove the grouse breasts.
300 ml (10 fl oz) Game Stock (see Tip on page 76)	Add, bring to the boil and season with salt and pepper. Simmer for about 15 minutes until the sauce has reduced a little. Add the breasts and reheat gently. They should be still pink.
15 ml (1 tablespoon) finely chopped fresh parsley	Sprinkle over the breasts and serve hot.

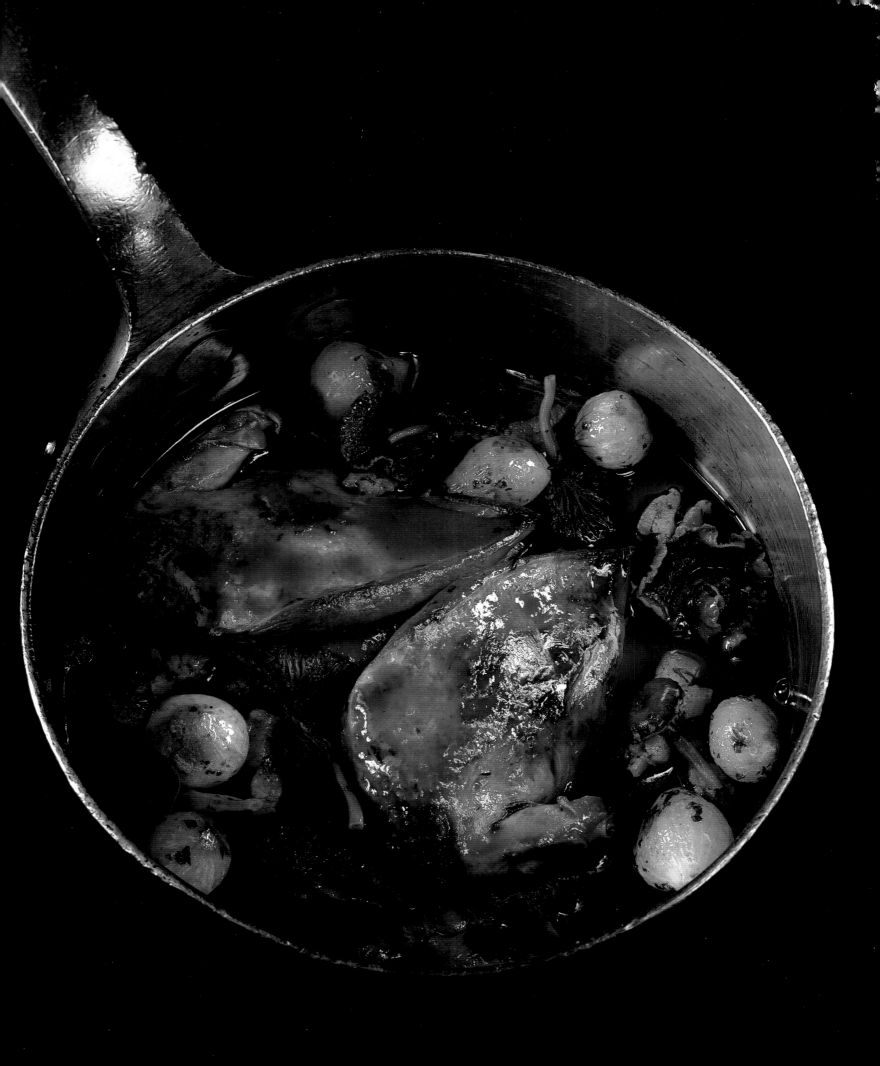

And that was how I came to invent the idea of the *Menu Surprise* – six featherlight courses, created using only the freshest ingredients straight from the market that day. The guest would not know what he was to eat until it appeared on the table. It was an entirely new concept and the secret was to offer a well balanced selection of dishes, that combined wonderful flavours, colours and textures, great creativity and of course first-class presentation. My chefs loved it because I asked them to create new dishes which motivated them to produce their very best; they could also present a complete and balanced *menu*, which would be much more representative of their culinary skills than a disparate selection of dishes. And as for the guests, they were presented with the most sumptuous meal, a truly modern banquet.

For instance we might start with marinated salmon garnished with tiny blinis, topped with a spoonful of caviar. To follow there would be a clear chicken consommé sprinkled with gold leaf, then steamed fillet of turbot or John Dory with a champagne sauce. This could be followed by a red wine granité and then a mignon of lamb. A selection of cheeses would be followed by something like an orange parfait with a raspberry coulis or yoghurt sauce.

The London *Evening Standard* dubbed it 'culinary blind dating', and that this concept appealed to many was apparent from the numbers that, over the next ten years, chose to be 'surprised'! Within a very short while, the menu had become so popular that you could almost guarantee that as many as 80 per cent of the guests would choose it.

For that re-opening of the Terrace restaurant, we created two new recipes which have since become

Passionfruit Soufflé

SERVES 4   OVEN: Moderate, 180°C/350°F/Gas 4

melted butter and sugar for the dish	Butter a 1.5 litre (2½ pint) glass, china or silver soufflé dish evenly and carefully. Brush it on in two even layers, chilling well in between. Dust with sugar.
3 egg yolks 100 g (4 oz) caster sugar 300 ml (10 fl oz) passionfruit juice (from 24–28 passionfruit, see Tip)	Beat the yolks with half the caster sugar and half of the passionfruit juice.
3 egg whites	Whisk with the remaining caster sugar until thick and creamy, as for meringues. Very carefully fold into the yolk mixture. Pour the mixture into the prepared dish, and give a fairly firm tap against the work surface to make it nice and smooth, with no air bubbles. Poach in a steaming bain-marie on top of the stove for 8–10 minutes. Remove from the bain-marie and bake in the preheated oven for 25–30 minutes.
20 g (¾ oz) caster sugar juice of ½ lemon	To make the sauce, boil up with the remaining passionfruit juice.
10 ml (2 teaspoons) cornflour or arrowroot, slaked in a little water	Add just enough to thicken the sauce. Bring to the boil.
icing sugar for dusting	Dust over the top of the soufflé when it is ready, and serve immediately. Serve the sauce separately, perhaps with a little whipped cream or natural yoghurt.

ANTON'S TIP

To make passionfruit juice, scoop seeds and flesh from half shells and place in a blender. Liquidise briefly to release the seeds from the juice, taking care not to break up the seeds. Strain.

modern 'classics' – Rendezvous de Fruits de Mer and our oyster sausage dish (overleaf).

Having established the Terrace menu, Udo and I turned our attention to the Grill Room, a robust, traditional restaurant, where we decided to re-focus on British cooking. Inspired by visits to the markets, we were determined to prove how good British cooking could be using only British products. We were to use nothing that might come from beyond British shores. For months I studied recipes from all over the British Isles with help from my *sous-chefs*, Paul Gayler (now chef at the new Lanesborough Hotel at Hyde Park Corner) and David Nicholls (now Executive Chef at the Ritz).

Those hours spent searching through hundreds of recipes were extraordinarily exhilarating. I was amazed to discover just how rich a seam of great dishes ran through the centuries, and was surprised that so many were now forgotten. Sadly hotels and restaurants had abandoned almost all but favourite roasts in their attempt to offer Continental cuisine, and of those that still cooked dishes like baked ham or silverside, the >

Rendezvous de Fruits de Mer

SERVES 4

4 large fresh scallops in their shells	Open with a small, strong knife by easing the flesh away from the debris and flat shell. Wash briefly but thoroughly, then separate the coral from the scallops. Cut each scallop in half horizontally and lay on a damp cloth with the coral.
12 fresh mussels in their shells	Scrub the shells and remove the beards. Place in a saucepan and heat gently until the mussels open. Discard any that remain closed. Reserve the juices and strain through muslin.
8 tiny squid	Remove the tentacles (reserve the bodies for another dish). Wash well and blanch in boiling water for 30 seconds. Drain and cool.
150 g (5 oz) fillet of turbot, skinned and cut into cubes of about 15 g (½ oz) each **12 scampi, removed from their shells** **8 raw Mediterranean prawns, heads and shells removed** **cayenne, salt and freshly ground pepper**	Season with cayenne, salt and pepper.
50 g (2 oz) leeks, white parts mainly	Thinly slice, and blanch in boiling salted water. Drain and cool.
400 ml (14 fl oz) Fish Stock (see page 156)	Heat to a gentle simmer with the mussel juices, then add the squid and prawns and poach for 1 minute. 　Add the scampi and turbot and poach for 1 minute. 　Add the leeks, mussels and scallop coral and poach for a further 30 seconds
4 sprigs fresh thyme	Add with the scallops and poach for yet another 30 seconds. 　Carefully arrange the fish in four individual soup dishes. 　Check the seasoning of the stock, and adjust to taste. Bring just to serving temperature, then pour over the fish and serve at once.

ANTON'S TIP

This can be served as either an hors d'oeuvre or a main course. It can utilise whatever seafood is in season or is best; poach according to size or thickness.

Oyster Sausages with Saffron and Ink Sauces

SERVES 4

200 g (7 oz) sea trout fillet, skinned, bones removed tweezers	To make the sausages, purée in a food processor. Chill in a bowl over ice.
100 g (4 oz) tofu salt and freshly ground pepper	Gradually beat into the trout purée, a little at a time. Season well, and chill until required.
24 oysters	Open and remove from their shells carefully, saving the liquid.
10 ml (2 teaspoons) finely snipped dill	Mix into the trout purée along with the oysters.
juice of ½ lemon	Use to season the mixture, along with some salt and pepper.
40–50 cm (16–20 in) sausage skins, soaked in water	Fill with the mixture of purée and whole oysters, doing so through a piping bag with a large nozzle. Tie with string to make four sausages. Chill until required.
400 ml (14 fl oz) Fish Stock (see page 156) 40 g (1½ oz) shallots, peeled and finely chopped	**To make the saffron sauce**, place in a pan and reduce by half by rapid boiling.
a few strands of saffron 100 g (4 oz) *fromage blanc*	Add and mix in well. Bring to the boil again, and pass through a fine sieve. Season to taste. Keep hot.
25 g (1 oz) shallots, peeled and finely chopped	**For the ink sauce**, sweat in a non-stick pan briefly.
500 g (18 oz) fresh squid *with ink*	Cut off heads, saving the remainder for another dish. Trim off beaks and eyes, then add heads and ink sacs to the shallots.
50 g (2 oz) tomatoes, diced	Add to the squid and sweat for a further 3–4 minutes.
300 ml (10 fl oz) Fish Stock (see page 156)	Add along with the oyster liquor, cover and simmer for 5 minutes. Pass through a fine sieve, boil up again, and season with salt and pepper. Keep hot. Poach the oyster sausages in water for about 3 minutes.
8 crayfish, poached for 2 minutes, tails removed	Sauté quickly in a non-stick pan. Season well and keep warm.

200 g (7 oz) tiny broccoli florets	Wash and blanch in boiling water for 15 seconds. Keep warm.
	  To serve, poach the oyster sausages in simmering water for about 3 minutes.
	  Pour the hot yellow saffron sauce on to half of four individual plates. Cover the other half of the plate with the hot black squid sauce. Place the oyster sausages in the middle of the two sauces, where the colours meet, and garnish with the crayfish and broccoli.

ANTON'S TIP

Instead of sausage skins, wrap the sausage mixture in culinary cling film, and poach as above. Remove before serving.

  Squid ink may now be bought in small sachets, and is easy to use.

majority had reduced these magnificent recipes to the indignity of gammon and pineapple or lifeless grey slivers of tired beef swimming in tasteless stock.

I couldn't wait to start work on recipes for suckling pig or braised oxtail, and selected these together with dishes like the hearty Lancashire hot-pot, simple poached haddock with parsley sauce, eel in green sauce, and a warming cock-a-leekie soup. Not forgetting, of course, the great British pies such as steak and kidney or shepherd's pie, which were hard to find well cooked except in someone's home. I even adapted that most traditional of British dishes – roast beef. I grilled double ribs, fat removed, with lots of fresh herbs, and cooked to order.

Naturally when it came to puddings we were spoiled for choice amongst the pies, crumbles, charlottes and steamed puddings. Britain has always been famous worldwide for her desserts, summer pudding and treacle tart among them. One that caught my eye particularly, however, was bread and butter pudding. Many of the recipes I tried produced a rather heavy result, but in my mind's eye, I could see it very light, with a texture almost like a soufflé. I reduced the quantity of bread and enriched the custard, which produced exactly what I wanted, a sweet, deliciously light pudding (see overleaf).

The reactions to both the new Terrace Restaurant and the revamped Grill Room were marvellous. Whereas it had been customary for guests at the hotel to eat out, they now booked ahead to make sure of being able to eat in. Indeed the Terrace Restaurant was consistently fully booked for years, so much so that guests would ring to make a reservation with the restaurant *before* booking their room at the hotel! It's difficult to describe how good that felt, not only for me but for all the chefs and everyone else involved with running the restaurants.

Two years after opening the Terrace, it was awarded its first Michelin star and two years later the second, making this the only hotel restaurant outside France to be given two stars. That was something indeed to be proud of.

The word soon spread and the restaurants were continually filled with famous faces. Lord McAlpine would eat in a private dining room in which he entertained at least three times a week. On each occasion I created a new menu, naming the main course after the guest of honour and not once was a menu repeated.

On another occasion, this time for the launch of a French cookery series by the *Observer* magazine, twenty-six different soufflés were prepared to be >

Grilled Rib of Angus Beef with Herbs

SERVES 4

1 prime rib of beef, approx. 1.4 kg (3 lb) in weight	Trim very well of excess fat. To ensure even cooking, get the butcher to cut the meat absolutely flat and level with the bone.
100 ml (3½ fl oz) olive oil 1 small sprig each of thyme and rosemary 4 sage leaves 8 basil leaves 2 garlic cloves, peeled and crushed	Mix together in a suitably sized dish and marinate the beef for 12 hours in a cool place.
salt and coarsely crushed black pepper	Remove the meat from the marinade, and season well. Heat a heavy iron frying pan, an oven-top ridged grill pan, or a conventional top-heat grill. Grill the beef on one side for about 7–8 minutes. Turn over and grill for another 7–8, according to how you like it cooked. Arrange on a suitable dish.
4 sprigs fresh rosemary, sautéed in a little butter a handful of fresh watercress	Use to garnish the beef.

ANTON'S TIP

It is important that while the beef is being marinated it is turned frequently.

To prevent the meat juices running out, the cooked beef should rest for 10 minutes before being carved into thin slices.

served at the same moment. But the *pièce de resistance* was that each soufflé represented a different letter of the alphabet from apple, banana, *champignon* to *zingara*, a classical Hungarian recipe made with ham, tongue and mushrooms.

It was in 1982 that I reacted to a new challenge. I had become increasingly aware of research that showed that heart disease, a major killer in the West, seemed to be directly linked to our consumption of saturated fat. Thus I started thinking about the possibility of creating a new style of cuisine that would avoid using less healthy ingredients such as fats, sugar and salt, and reduce the amount of alcohol. Personally I have always been careful with my health, partly from being a keen sportsman which made me aware of nutritional values, but largely because I felt that perhaps if my mother's diet had been more healthy, she might still be alive today.

Although I knew that a lot of people would greet my ideas with remarks like 'How can one eat without butter and cream?', I was convinced that it was possible to cook well without relying upon these less healthy ingredients. Drawing on my experience of other cuisines, such as the Japanese which uses no dairy produce, I knew that there were indeed other ways. I sought to create a cuisine dedicated to combining the ideals of 'good food' and 'food that is good for you', two things that had until now seemed mutually exclusive. The idea that one swung like a pendulum from indulgence in red meat coated with rich sauces and puddings served with lashings of cream to the other extreme of starving oneself with plain salads with no dressings and a dollop of cottage cheese was, I believed, lacking in imagination. I was determined to create a happy balance, a cuisine which offered mouth-watering recipes that were not laden with salt, sugar and fat yet provided the fresh fruit, vegetables, proteins and dietary fibre so often lacking in a Western diet.

I refused to accept that eggs and butter were essential and irreplaceable. With a bit of imagination, I knew >

Bread and Butter Pudding

SERVES 4   OVEN: Moderate, 160°C/325°F/Gas 3

40 g (1½ oz) unsalted butter	Use a little to grease a large oval pie dish.
6 small soft bread rolls, thinly sliced	Use the rest of the butter to spread over the bread slices. Arrange these buttered slices in the base of the dish.
500 ml (17 fl oz) each of milk and double cream **a little salt** **1 vanilla pod, split**	Bring to the boil gently together in a pan.
6 large eggs **250 g (9 oz) vanilla sugar**	Mix together until pale. Gradually add the milk and cream mixture to the eggs, stirring well to amalgamate.
25 g (1 oz) sultanas, soaked in water and drained	Add to the bread in the dish, along with the milk mixture, which has been passed through a sieve. The bread will float to the top. Place the dish in a bain-marie on top of folded newspaper, and pour in enough hot water to come halfway up the sides of the dish. Poach carefully in the preheated oven for 45–50 minutes. When the pudding is ready, it should wobble very slightly in the middle. Remove from the oven and cool a little.
100 g (4 oz) apricot glaze **icing sugar to dust**	Brush a thin coating of the warm glaze over the top of the pudding, then dust with icing sugar.

ANTON'S TIP

To make vanilla sugar, simply store a vanilla pod in a canister of caster sugar; the pod will imbue the sugar with its flavour. To make apricot glaze, melt some apricot jam, sieve and use the warm sweet liquid to give a shine.

The essence of Cuisine Naturelle – no cream, no butter, no oil, no alcohol. . .

that I would be able to create some kind of healthy alternative that could also provide the textures and tastes enjoyed in the West. It was by experimenting that I learnt ways in which low-fat yoghurt, *fromage blanc* and *tofu* (soya bean curd) could be used instead of cream or eggs for creating, for example, a mayonnaise. This could be flavoured with finely chopped fresh herbs, a good alternative to salt. Delicious sauces were created by reducing meat, fish and vegetable stocks, or by sieving or puréeing colourful vegetables and fruits. None of these needed any additional cream, butter or alcohol.

The invention of non-stick surfaces, a by-product of the space industry, helped enormously. Using the best non-stick pan one could fry with no fat and yet without compromising the flavour. For example, a dish like *Rösti*, usually fried in bacon fat, worked wonderfully when fried directly on the pan until golden brown. They would then be finished in a hot oven, and often shredded potato was mixed with shredded parsnips, to give a slightly sweet taste. Again, instead of frying onions and garlic in oil or butter for a sauce, we demonstrated that they could simply be sweated in a dry frying pan.

I tried to keep the recipes as simple as possible, >

Steamed Halibut with Courgettes and Tomato Vinaigrette

SERVES 4

4 × 150 g (5 oz) halibut fillets salt and freshly ground pepper	Season the fillets with salt and pepper to taste.

200–250 g (7–9 oz) medium courgettes	Top, tail and score using a cannelle knife. Cut into thin slices.
	  Arrange the slices on top of the halibut fillets in neat overlapping rows. Season gently.
	  Place the fish in the top part of a steamer and steam for about 5–7 minutes, depending on the thickness of the fish.

250 ml (9 fl oz) tomato *concassée* (see page 35)	Meanwhile, warm through gently in a pan.
100 ml (3½ fl oz) reduced Fish Stock (see page 156) 60 ml (4 tablespoons) balsamic vinegar 8 basil leaves, cut into fine strips	Mix together and add to the tomato for the vinaigrette, with salt and pepper to taste. Divide the vinaigrette between four plates and arrange the fish and courgettes on top.
4 sprigs fresh thyme	Use as a garnish, and serve immediately.

ANTON'S TIP

Other fish can be cooked similarly, according to what is available in the market.

For the reduced Fish stock, start off with about 200 ml (7 fl oz). For a non Cuisine Naturelle recipe, you could use olive oil in the vinaigrette instead of the stock.

partly because this ensures the flavour shines through, but also because I wanted these recipes and this new way of cooking to be available to everyone, not just those who could afford to eat at hotels and restaurants.

Every weekend I experimented in the kitchen at home, and the very first recipe that I created within these new parameters was fish served on top of two sauces of red and yellow peppers. The sauces glowed with the natural colours of the vegetables and contrasted beautifully with the whiteness of the fresh fish which had been steamed for just a few minutes so retaining its texture. The halibut dish on page 120 displays many of the central principles of Cuisine Naturelle.

I found that without the muting effect of cream, butter or alcohol, the natural flavours shone through much more. Similarly, using healthier cooking methods such as steaming, poaching and grilling conserved not only the nutrients but also the taste, colour and aroma of the food. These dishes were more honest and more delicate than the traditional way of cooking, but above all they were more natural, and that was why it seemed fitting to call this new style of cooking *Cuisine Naturelle*.

Once I had formed the outline for the idea and was

building up the recipes, I turned for expert dietary advice from Dr Janet Gale, a lecturer in health and social welfare at the Open University. In all we worked on these ideas over two years, and in 1985 the book of *Cuisine Naturelle* was ready to be published.

To coincide with publication about a third of the dishes on the restaurant menus were devoted to the principles of *Cuisine Naturelle* and distinguished with a 'CN' beside their name. My main concern, however, was to get the ideas in that book across to a much wider audience so I was delighted that the book sold well.

Not long after, the BBC *Food and Drink* programme challenged me to go with a film crew to cook a meal for a family living in a council house in Sheffield. John Willcox, a lorry driver for the local council, usually cooked the Sunday lunch for his family of six. Having found out that their favourite lunch was roast beef with Yorkshire pudding, I suggested that we waited until we saw what was on offer at the market. My budget was £10.

Sheffield has a large covered market where we bought two chickens. This would be enough for a fricassée which I decided to flavour with ginger. Next we bought some vegetables. I showed them how to test an onion by feeling for firmness and then suggested we saved money by buying a couple of slightly bruised green and red peppers for the sauce. Cabbage was very inexpensive so we bought that, and I decided to cook it with a little chopped bacon and onion. Finally I bought eggs, cream, milk and sugar and used some stale bread for a bread and butter pudding.

John and his wife Margaret watched as I cooked, and I think they were most surprised by how little time the vegetables took to cook, some 4–5 minutes. The overall result, however, was a great success. Margaret, who had never eaten garlic or green peppers, was won over to these new tastes, and the bread and butter pudding was so popular that their youngest grandchild, who usually refused pudding, asked for a second helping!

I was delighted with the response and was only too pleased when the BBC suggested that I should go back a few months later so that John could cook lunch for me. This time he made a *carbonnade de boeuf* and Margaret prepared her favourite Irish dish, mashed cauliflower, followed by the new family favourite – bread and butter pudding. I thought the stew was very good, though I suggested that as he had found such good beef, he should have been able to reduce the cooking time. (I think many in the UK have a tendency to over-cook good quality meat.) But the real surprise

With John and Margaret Willcox at Sheffield Market, filming for the BBC *Food and Drink* programme.

With the kitchen brigade at the Dorchester. On my left is Udo Schlentrich, and behind is my secretary, Sylvia Baumann.

came when I tasted the pudding. It was perfect. I was really moved because he had obviously paid so much attention that first time since I hadn't left a recipe.

I wasn't the only person who was affected by those two visits to Sheffield. The BBC told me they had received 65,000 letters from viewers who wanted the recipes! It was heartening news as I have always loved passing on my knowledge. Meanwhile, the reputation of both the restaurants and the kitchen at the Dorchester spread, and we now had a waiting list of over 650 chefs from all over the world who wanted to come and work with us. I couldn't have wished for better proof that my attempt to run a happy kitchen worked.

However tough things had been at the beginning, I now had a good solid brigade of eighty-five, over 90 per cent of whom were British. I had reduced the number of chefs by fifty, although I'd added two kitchens, and had gained two Michelin stars. All the chefs were full of enthusiasm for their work and as they gave to the kitchen, so in my turn I tried to help give them the best training and career advice that I could. I

feel like a proud father whose children have gone out and now hold important positions in some of the best kitchens in the world.

The Dorchester kitchens are now in the hands of Willy Elsener, one of those who had worked with me.

Chapter Eight

Mosimann's

ORIGINALLY I HAD NEVER THOUGHT TO LEAVE THE DORCHESTER, BUT AFTER TWELVE YEARS, I WAS APPROACHING FORTY, I HAD ACHIEVED EVERY POSSIBLE AWARD THERE WAS TO ACHIEVE, AND I NEEDED A NEW CHALLENGE. THERE HAD ALSO BEEN SEVERAL OTHER MANAGERIAL CHANGES SINCE UDO LEFT, WHICH WEREN'T NECESSARILY GOOD FOR THE HOTEL.

FOR INSTANCE, I REMEMBER ONE NEW MANAGER DECIDING THAT HE WANTED TO PUT THE FOOD AND BEVERAGE CONTROLLER IN CHARGE OF RECEIVING THE FOOD DELIVERIES. THIS WAS INEVITABLY GOING TO IRRITATE THE WELL-ESTABLISHED SYSTEM IN THE KITCHEN WHERE ONE OF THE *SOUS* CHEFS HAD BEEN DOING THE JOB FOR FIFTEEN YEARS. HE HAD ESTABLISHED AN EXCELLENT RAPPORT WITH THE PRODUCERS AND SUPPLIERS, AND COULD BE RELIED UPON TO SELECT THE FINEST PRODUCE. HOWEVER, RATHER THAN START OFF ON THE WRONG FOOT WITH THIS NEW MANAGER, BY TELLING HIM JUST HOW UNWISE I CONSIDERED HIS IDEA, I DECIDED TO TRUST FATE.

ON THE FIRST MONDAY MORNING I ASKED THE CONTROLLER TO MAKE QUITE SURE THAT WHEN THE FRUITERER ARRIVED, HE SELECTED ONLY RIPE MELONS. HE STARED AT ME WITH AN EXPRESSION OF COMPLETE INCOMPREHENSION — HE OBVIOUSLY HADN'T THE FIRST IDEA OF HOW TO TELL WHETHER THE FRUIT WAS RIPE OR NOT.

When Tuesday came we were expecting a delivery of lobsters. I asked the same man to make sure the lobsters were Scottish, alive and, of course, female only. This time he stared at me as though I had come from the moon. He carefully put his pencil in his pocket, tucked his notebook under his arm and then dashed back upstairs to his boss. That, thankfully, was the end of that!

There were several other such confrontations, but the last straw came just after I had learnt that we had been awarded our second Michelin star. Naturally I was delighted by the news. This was the highest award a hotel restaurant can achieve, and for two weeks I was really excited and flying high. But I came down to earth with a rude bump. When I showed the new *Guide Michelin* to the latest general manager, instead of a great beam spreading over his face, he just looked blankly at me and asked, 'What's that?'

It was then that I asked for a three-month sabbatical leave. I had very seriously to plan my next professional move. Rumours had already been circulating that I might be leaving the Dorchester, and I was offered some marvellous positions abroad. However, I had made some tremendous friends, and I didn't want to leave England. In terms of a chef's career, there was no higher I could go in a hotel, so what next?

A private dining club seemed like the perfect solution. I

would at last be able to create my own restaurant. To cook for people I knew, for old friends and, I hoped, new ones, would be more satisfying and enjoyable than cooking for a stream of unknown faces. The joy of my work comes from being able to cook for people I know, to be able to give them their favourites dishes or cook something they rarely have. I want to know their likes and dislikes, their favourite tables and to be able to create a surprise for a special occasion.

But the other great advantage of a club over a hotel would lie in being able to ensure that everything ran as I wished. It would be a hymn to perfection – so much easier to achieve in a private club than a hotel. It was going to be a move from grand opera to conducting a little chamber music.

I got as far as making an offer for a club I'd seen, with financial help from several friends. That subsequently fell through – and thankfully, for I was soon to find the ideal venue.

I'll never forget the first time I saw the old Belfry Club in London's Belgravia. It was in October 1987, and I had been taken there for dinner by a friend, Dr Rainer Kahrmann. Having heard quite a lot about it, I had assumed it would be very modern so I was completely taken aback to find that it still looked like a church. From the outside, wonderful gothic spires and gargoyles stared down at passers-by; inside the dining-room was open to a high vaulted ceiling from which praying angels looked down. All the original moulding remained, as did the brilliant stained-glass and leaded windows.

As we sat talking over dinner, the place grew on me. I started to imagine myself running up and down the stairs and talking to the guests. That night I hardly slept for thinking of what I would do with the club if it were mine. It was a very special building, I knew, but only later did I discover quite what an interesting history it had.

Built in 1830 as a church, it was leased by the Presbyterian Church of Scotland until 1923 when the congregation had almost disappeared and the church reverted to the Grosvenor Estate. The next tenant was an extraordinary woman, a Mrs Zoe Oakley Maund who converted it into a private home with eight bedrooms and six fitted bathrooms. She removed the altar and pews and converted the nave into a dining-room which was overlooked by the drawing-room in the old gallery. She also installed a new organ.

Lady Caillard, as she became after her marriage in 1927, was fascinated by spiritualism and the occult, and after her husband's death in 1930 she invented an instrument she called the 'communigraph' through which her

**Looking down into the
restaurant and across to
the bar from the wine
cellar at Mosimann's.**

dead husband sent her the material for a book named *A New Conception of Love*. There were regular meetings and the Belfry was famous for the séances held there in the early thirties. But in 1935, Lady Caillard went to join her husband and the next day the London newspapers carried a photograph of the Belfry, as she had called it, with its cross, lit by blue neon lights.

In 1945 the Belfry Club was founded by members of the Royal Air Force and it remained a RAF club until 1954 when it was bought by Joseph Vecchi, a well-known restaurateur. He turned the Belfry into a dining

club which it remained, albeit changing hands several times.

To me the Belfry had a unique atmosphere which I felt was rather stifled by the heavy, dark red classical decor. I visualised a much lighter interior which I knew would transform it from an interesting but rather gloomy and old-fashioned gentlemen's club, into something really special.

My decision to act as fast as possible on the Belfry was strengthened by the knowledge that the Dorchester, built in 1930, was due for major repairs. There was even talk of closing it for two years whilst the work was done.

Anxious to make my move before any such upheavals, I re-contacted the friends who had offered financial help previously, and they immediately agreed. That was all I needed to know. Now confident of my backers, I wasted no time in picking up the telephone.

The first time I called, the owners declared the club was definitely not for sale, but if they thought they were going to put me off that easily, they were wrong! There is a price for everything after all, and sure enough, several offers, phone calls and meetings later, we had a price. The tension made the time drag dreadfully, but in fact the negotiations had taken less than a fortnight.

Having put so much energy into making this happen, it came as a great surprise and pleasure to at last be able to toast the future in champagne. But of course it was incredibly frustrating, because now came the waiting. First there was the question of handing in my notice. The news came as a great shock to the Dorchester management, despite the rumours that had been circulating. With discussions over, I left the kitchen for the last time on Monday March 31st. On Tuesday April 1st 1988 I started at the Belfry.

Despite the excitement, I was very sad to leave all my good friends. There were many goodbyes and it felt, after so long, as though a chapter of my life had closed. But the future lay waiting and I was ready to move on. My plan was to let the club continue to run for three months along the same lines as before whilst I got to know how it worked. I had found a new chef, Ralph Bürgin, my former right-hand man at the Terrace restaurant, who had subsequently moved back to Germany. (He is now cooking at the Carnelian Room, Bankers Club, in San Rafael, California.) The rest of the brigade was made up of half of the existing chefs and some new faces, but otherwise the only change that needed to be made at this point was simply to improve the quality of the cooking. >

Tomato, Mozzarella and Basil Terrine

SERVES 4

12–14 large ripe plum tomatoes	Cut to fit a small, deep terrine dish. Hold a tomato upright, stem uppermost, and cut down thick slices off the four sides, leaving a square core in the middle (discard this). This will give you four roughly rectangular 1.5 cm (½ in) thick slices. Cut all the tomatoes similarly. Flatten the slices gently under the palm of your hand and trim into neat rectangles.
500 g (18 oz) Mozzarella cheese	Cut into similar slices, and trim into neat rectangles.
a large bunch of fresh basil	Wash, gently pat dry, and pick off the leaves. Line the terrine with cling film. Place a layer of slices of tomato, skin side down, into the base of the terrine. Try to make the slices fit exactly to give a neat final effect.
salt and freshly ground pepper	Season well and add a layer of Mozzarella slices, followed by a layer of basil leaves. Keep adding layers in the same order, finishing with a layer of tomato. Cover with cling film and a flat piece of card cut to fit the top of the terrine exactly. Place a light weight on top and chill for several hours. This will help the layers stick together. To serve, unmould carefully on to a chopping board, and slice into thick individual slices.
4 sprigs fresh basil good olive oil and balsamic vinegar	Use to garnish each plate.

I wasn't ready to wear my own chef's jacket yet – that time would come – as the style of food served at the club was not mine. The orchestra was not ready for me to conduct. But I was hard at work in my head, inventing and creating many new ideas as to the food I should like to cook there. I wanted it to be international and modern, a style of cooking that would reflect all those long years and all those invaluable influences.

Switzerland, my home country, would be represented by my new ideas on *Rösti*, by some chicken recipes and

fruit purées and tarts. There was a rich seam there to be taken advantage of. Italy too had been such a major influence, and I knew my risotto would be popular (as indeed it is!). I could see many possibilities in pasta dishes, and in adapting the idea of the classic pizza. I had loved the glorious vegetables in Italy, and determined to serve them simply, perhaps grilled, or in a terrine of some sort.

I had learned so much about fish in Montreal, Japan Scandinavia and Belgium that I knew I would be offering *tataki*, *sushi*, fish *tartares*, *gravadlax*, clam and oyster >

Leek, Mussel and Squid Tortino

SERVES 4   OVEN: Very hot, 240°C/475°F/Gas 9

10 g (⅓ oz) fresh yeast 85–100 ml (3–3½ fl oz) lukewarm milk	Dissolve the yeast in the milk.
75 g (3 oz) each of wheatmeal and white unbleached bread flours	Sift into a bowl and make a well in the centre.
60 ml (4 tablespoons) olive oil a pinch of salt	Add to the well along with the yeast milk, and mix evenly together. Knead for a few minutes. Form the dough into a ball and place in an oiled bowl. Cover with clingfilm and leave to rise in a warm place for 1 hour.
about 24 mussels, scrubbed 100 ml (3½ fl oz) Fish Stock (see page 156) 50 ml (2 fl oz) white wine	Meanwhile, make the topping. Heat the mussels through in the liquid in a covered pan until they open, a few minutes only. Keep to one side to cool a little, then remove the flesh from the shells.
100 ml (3½ fl oz) olive oil about 450 g (1 lb) young leeks, sliced thinly on the diagonal and rinsed	Heat the oil in a pan and stir-fry the leek rings for a few minutes to soften.
about 225 g (8 oz) fresh squid, cleaned and cut into rings	Add and stir-fry for a few more minutes. Remove from the oil using a slotted spoon. When the dough has risen, knead again and roll out into one large (or four smaller) pizza shape(s) of about 3mm (⅛ in) thick. Place on oiled baking sheets and gently raise the edges.
250 g (9 oz) tomato *concassée* (see page 35)	Spread over the base of the dough circle(s).
100 g (4 oz) Mozzarella cheese, thinly sliced	Top with the cheese, shelled mussels, leek and squid rings.
a good handful of dill sprigs salt and freshly ground pepper	Sprinkle over the topping and season to taste. Bake in the preheated oven for 20 minutes.

ANTON'S TIP

Instead of the tomato *concassée*, you could use a good home-made tomato sauce, and/or you could mix in some finely chopped sun-dried tomatoes in oil. You could vary the topping as well, according to taste and seasonal produce; filo pastry could also be used as a base.

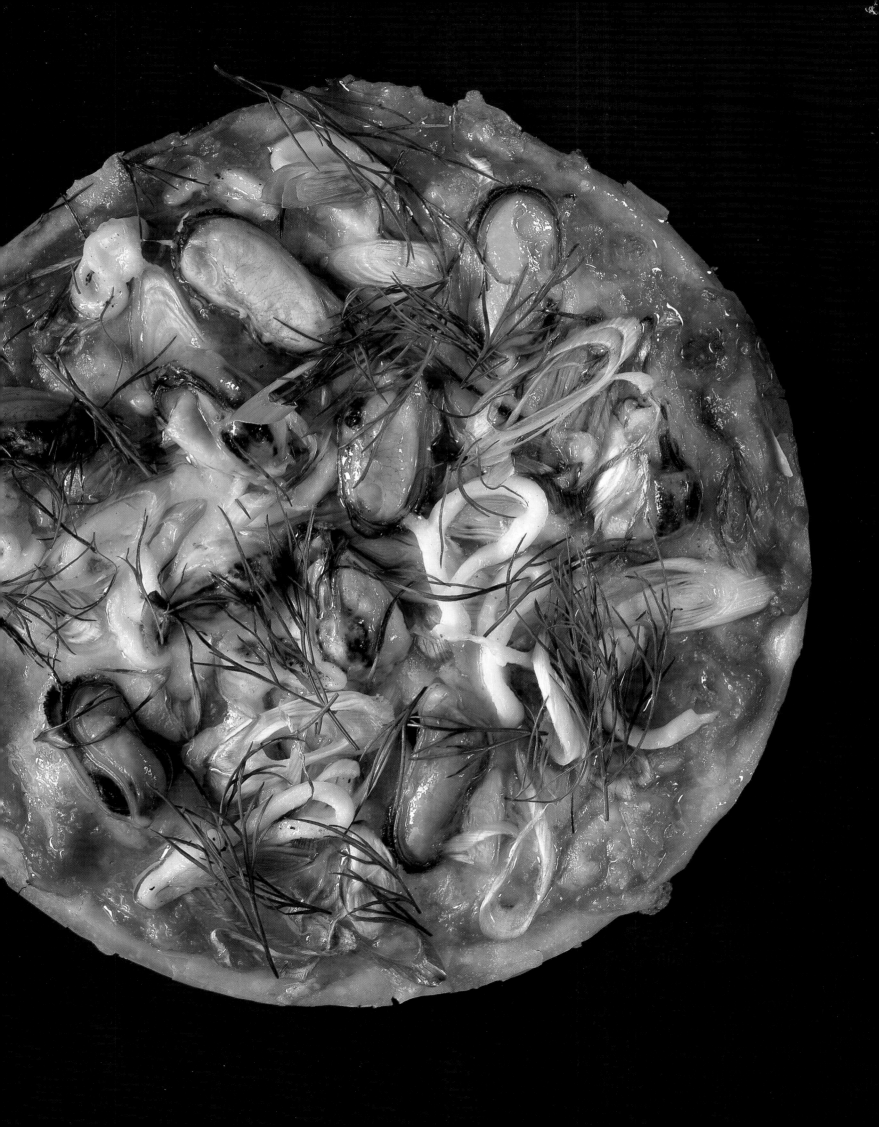

The Wedgwood Room in the club is light, bright and predominantly Wedgwood blue. Its stained-glass windows look down over the restaurant and the bar gallery, and on the walls are some of the original designs for early Wedgwood porcelain. It seats thirty.

dishes. I thought an English inspired fish cake might not go amiss either! There were many Japanese flavourings that I had experimented with and knew could complement other than fish – chicken and beef, for instance.

And Britain, of course, where I had been working for the past twelve years, had introduced me to many new ideas, marvellous local ingredients such as beef, salmon and cheese, and to many challenges. I hoped my bread and butter pudding would be popular (indeed it's become almost a trademark recipe), but I was even thinking of reworking the classic British Christmas mince pie!

During those first thoughts of the food I should serve, I was busy redesigning the club. I came in every morning and studied the place. I looked at the arrangement of the building and considered ways of improving both the layout of the dining-room and kitchen, as well as using more of the office space. I wondered around and sat in each room trying to gauge to what use it could be best put.

The bar, for instance, was hidden away in a dark corner at the back of the dining-room. This meant that guests >

Marinated Grilled Vegetables

SERVES 4

85 ml (3 fl oz) olive oil 3 sprigs fresh thyme 1 garlic clove, peeled and halved	Heat the oil together gently with the thyme and garlic, to perfume the oil. Leave to cool and infuse.
1 medium aubergine salt and freshly ground pepper	Trim and cut lengthwise into four thick slices. Sprinkle with salt and leave to drain in a colander, about 15 minutes. Pat dry.
1 large Spanish onion, peeled 2 large firm tomatoes 2 large courgettes, topped and tailed 2 medium green or red peppers	Cut the vegetables in half, the onion and tomatoes horizontally, the courgettes lengthwise, the peppers from top to bottom. Seed the latter.
4 large field mushrooms	Wipe with a damp cloth. Brush the vegetables all over with the perfumed olive oil – you could use the thyme itself to do this. Grill on both sides on a barbecue or under a preheated grill until cooked: the pepper halves, aubergine and onion slices will take about 8–10 minutes; the courgettes about 5–6; the tomatoes and mushrooms seconds only. Remove to a platter, skinning the pepper first if preferred. Drizzle with more olive oil and season to taste with salt and pepper.
30 ml (2 tablespoons) roughly cut basil leaves	Sprinkle over the vegetables. Serve warm or cold.

ANTON'S TIP

Different vegetables can be used, according to the season, as the dish is very flexible. Serve as a refreshing first course.

were constantly walking between the tables, upsetting those already seated and getting in the way of the waiters. It would obviously be much better to move the bar upstairs where it would be bathed by the light streaming through the stained-glass windows. And if we hung a large mirror on the wall behind it, the effect would be even greater. Already I could see the rows of gleaming glass decanters filled with liqueurs and golden whiskies. By building a new staircase and creating a balcony there would be enough room to have tables and comfortable arm-chairs for guests to sit upstairs and enjoy a leisurely drink before eating.

We also decided that it would be a nice idea to have the wine cellar in the bar area so that guests could walk in and choose their own wines. It also looks very good, and over the years we have saved the ends of the best wine boxes >

Sesame Chicken with Warm Noodles

SERVES 4

30 ml (2 tablespoons) sherry vinegar 20 ml (4 teaspoons) balsamic vinegar 5 ml (1 teaspoon) caster sugar 100 ml (3½ fl oz) light soy sauce 60 ml (4 tablespoons) sesame oil 40 ml (1½ fl oz) light olive oil 2 small red chilli peppers, seeded and finely cut salt and freshly ground pepper	Mix together for the dressing, and season to taste with salt and pepper.
1 garlic clove, peeled 2 slices fresh ginger, peeled	Chop together very finely.
30 ml (2 tablespoons) olive oil 200 g (7 oz) chicken breast, skinned and cut into strips (from a maize-fed or free-range bird)	Heat half of the olive oil in a sauté pan and add half of the garlic and ginger mixture and the chicken. Stir-fry for about 3–4 minutes. Remove and keep to one side.
200 g (7 oz) beansprouts, washed and dried	Cook briefly in the remaining oil, with the remaining garlic and ginger. Place in a large bowl.
100 g (4 oz) mangetouts 50 g (2 oz) carrots, peeled	String the mangetouts, cut into fine strips and blanch. Cut the carrots into long fine strips. Season separately with salt, pepper and a little of the dressing.
400 g (14 oz) fresh fine Chinese egg noodles	Cook in a large pan of boiling water. Stir to separate. This takes only a few minutes – be careful not to overcook. Put into a colander and strain well, shaking off any excess liquid. Place in the bowl with the beansprouts. Pour in the remaining dressing.
25 g (1 oz) fresh coriander, roughly cut	Add, and toss the noodle mixture well together. Take a large fork and wind the noodles around it. Mound these on to individual plates. Garnish with the mangetouts, carrots and chicken.
15 ml (1 tablespoon) each of white sesame seeds, toasted, and black sesame seeds	Sprinkle over each mound of noodles, vegetables and chicken, and serve.

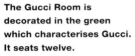

and used them to cover the ceiling.

But there was so much to do. Every day I had meetings and more meetings with architects and designers, at which we talked through every last detail, from the colour of the wallpaper to exactly which shade to bleach the wood. For three weeks we considered, testing the various samples of bleached wood against different wallpapers so that I could see how they looked at eight o'clock in the morning, at five in the afternoon and at ten at night.

During this time I had another book published, my *Fish Cuisine*, which meant I was having to divide my time dashing from one place to the next. One minute I was in a BBC studio recording my Desert Island Discs with Sue Lawley (my luxury was a steamer), and later I would be deep in discussions with carpenters. Life was certainly hectic, but I was fired by my determination to get the club ready.

It was a very exciting year, during which I was awarded the Chevalier de l'Ordre du Mérite Agricole from the Min-

istère d'Agricole in France for my culinary work. But however important the event, I couldn't keep away from the Belfry.

One of the main structural difficulties was the pulling out of the staircases leading from the kitchen to the dining-room. They were so narrow that the waiters could only carry two plates upstairs at a time, so we obviously had to have them widened where possible. As for the kitchen, this was going to be completely rebuilt, which involved hours of careful studying. I needed to rationalise the positions of the hot kitchen, the cold kitchen and the pastry section, so as to minimise the amount of time spent walking from one area to another and to the larder, which needed to be as close as possible to all three.

Once I had formulated the rough idea in my head, I had a plan drawn up which we then used to build a life-size model from cardboard boxes in a large room upstairs. In my opinion the only real way to design a workable kitchen is to have a menu in your mind and then to imagine you >

The Gucci Room is decorated in the green which characterises Gucci. It seats twelve.

Garden Leaves with Farm-Raised Chicken and 'Crackling'

SERVES 4   OVEN: Hot, 220°C/435°F/Gas 7

4 × 100g (4 oz) maize-fed or free-range chicken breasts	Remove the skin from the chicken breasts and keep aside. Trim the chicken of bones and any fat.
100 ml (3½ fl oz) natural yoghurt 2 strips lemon peel juice of ½ lemon 1 spring onion, cut 2 slices fresh ginger, finely peeled and crushed 1 garlic clove, peeled and crushed	Mix together in a dish, then marinate the chicken in this overnight.
30 ml (2 tablespoons) olive oil salt and freshly ground pepper	Heat the oil in a frying pan. Remove excess marinade from the chicken breasts, then season them well. Pan-fry in the hot oil until cooked and golden, about 5 minutes per side. Cut the chicken skin into pieces about 2.5 cm (1 in) square, sprinkle with salt, and bake in the hot oven until golden and crisp. Drain well on kitchen paper.
30 ml (2 tablespoons) Hoisin (barbecue) sauce	Brush over the chicken breasts, and keep warm with the crisp skins.
250 g (9 oz) mixed salad leaves about 60 ml (4 tablespoons) vinaigrette made with balsamic vinegar	Toss together gently, then arrange on four plates. Slice the warm, well seasoned chicken breasts and place over the salad. Serve immediately, garnished with the chicken 'crackling'.

Jersey Royal Potato Salad

SERVES 4

300 g (10 oz) Jersey Royal new potatoes salt and freshly ground pepper	Boil in salted water for about 15 minutes, or until just done. Cut in half and season with salt and pepper.
½ cucumber	Peel and cut in half lengthwise. Remove the seeds. Cut flesh into crescents or small dice, then sprinkle lightly with salt and place in a colander to drain.
200 g (7 oz) tomatoes	Core, then cut into quarters and seed. Cut each quárter in half again.
15 ml (1 tablespoon) grain mustard 150 g (5 oz) Greek yoghurt 15 ml (1 tablespoon) sherry vinegar	Mix together in a serving bowl.
1 bunch radishes, washed, trimmed and quartered 1 bunch spring onions, trimmed and finely cut 15 ml (1 tablespoon) finely chopped parsley 15 ml (1 tablespoon) finely cut dill	Add to the dressing, along with the drained cucumber, the tomato and potatoes. Mix well. Correct the seasoning and serve.

ANTON'S TIP

This salad is an ideal accompaniment for warm fish dishes.

The newly decorated Harvey Nichols Room, at the apex of the club. It seats fifty.

are actually preparing the dishes. By doing this step by step, actually calling out orders to the chefs, whom I had borrowed from the real kitchen, we could make sure no elements had been overlooked.

I had engaged a kitchen designer cum architect and I was clearly driving him crazy with all my checking and counter-checking. He kept insisting that I needn't worry, that he had designed plenty of kitchens and knew exactly what he was doing. That might have been so, but I wasn't taking any risks. I had worked in more kitchens than most people and had never come across a perfect one. I was *dreaming* kitchens before we finished, but at last I was satisfied and flew to Switzerland to show my plans to a company of kitchen people there who had assured me they would be able to build the kitchen to a tight deadline.

Finally I felt we were ready for action and on the last

Beef Tournedos with Sweet Peppers and Black Bean Sauce

SERVES 4

4 small beef tournedos, cut from the fillet, about 160 g (5½ oz) each	Trim the tournedos well.
1 each of medium red, yellow and green peppers	Sear in the oven or over a flame, then skin. Remove the cores, seeds and ribs and cut into even strips.
20 ml (4 teaspoons) fermented black beans	Rinse with cold water and squeeze dry. Put half into a mortar.
2 small garlic cloves, peeled 2.5 cm (1 in) cube fresh ginger, peeled and roughly cut	Grind with the black beans in the mortar until smooth.
salt and freshly ground pepper 15 ml (1 tablespoon) olive oil	Season the tournedos then pan-fry in the oil for 2–3 minutes on each side. Remove from the pan and keep warm. Sauté the pepper strips quickly in the oil remaining in the pan. Season and keep warm. Remove any excess oil from the pan.
50 ml (2 fl oz) red wine 200 ml (7 fl oz) Brown Veal Stock (see page 157), reduced by half	Deglaze the pan with the wine, then add the reduced veal stock and black bean paste. Stir together for a few minutes, then add the remaining whole black beans. Coat the tournedos with the sauce and top with the sweet pepper strips.
30 ml (2 tablespoons) fresh coriander leaves	Use to garnish the beef and peppers. Serve immediately.

Sunday in June we held a great party. It was a farewell to the Belfry but the beginnings of Mosimann's. The atmosphere was alive. The team was in place and we were ready to go!

The guests left at eleven p.m. and at midnight the removal men arrived. They took everything out. The tables and chairs, the cutlery, plates and glasses and all the kitchen equipment, literally everything went, so that we could start from scratch. At seven o'clock sharp the following morning the builders moved in. We had up to sixty-five people working on site and exactly three months to get everything ready.

Each day I walked round getting to know all the workmen. I chatted to the plasterers and the carpenters, listening to them as they described what they were doing, and praising their work. If the job gets done on time, I told them, you can have a meal on the house. It was a question of using the carrot, rather than the stick! Neither was I ever afraid of getting my hands dirty. On the contrary I was only too ready to lend a hand where it was needed and day by day, with everyone helping, the work progressed.

The Swiss kitchen design company lived up to their reputation, arriving on the very day they had promised and fitting each item perfectly into place. The kitchen was made of stainless steel and the ovens heated by a combination of convection and steam. We also had a large steamer and a special bread-baking oven so that everything could be made in the kitchen. The great advantage of choosing an induction stove was that it never feels very hot which would prevent the temperature in the kitchen from becoming uncomfortable. Even the ceiling was special. Rather than the old-fashioned ducting system, I chose air-conditioning which is extremely efficient, presents no cleaning problems and has the added bonus of looking fantastic.

Upstairs, we had decided that as well as the main dining-room, we should have several other rooms that could be used for private functions. How could we make these really special? I thought it would be a good idea to invite three companies involved in the world of design to sponsor their own rooms in the club. As a result we created three fabulous rooms for Gucci, Tiffany and Wedgwood, each of which we decorated in the most sumptuous manner to reflect their individual inspiration. Since then we

The Alfa Romeo Room, in which there is a spectacular table which seats ten, and early car designs on the walls.

have substituted Harvey Nichols for Tiffany and created a new room for Alfa Romeo. The chef's dining-room, with a window overlooking the kitchen, has been sponsored by Bulthaup and can also be used for private parties.

Throughout the club, the walls are decorated with masses of pictures, cartoons and memorabilia, things that have appealed me over the years, including my collection of old menus. Some were given to me, others I bought at auction. I've got the 1921 Christmas menu from the Savoy, a dinner for a Russian royal wedding and plenty of others from wonderful old hotels like the Cecil and Claridges.

I also have a marvellous collection of old cookery books from all over the world. The start of this collection were 1,500 books that had belonged to Adelrich Furrer who had sadly died only a few months after I started at the Dorchester. In his will he had asked his wife to give me first offer to buy them. Even though I didn't have the money at the time, I borrowed it from the bank, and I'm so glad I did. As I have been adding to them ever since, there are now around 4,000 books, many of which we used when we were researching old recipes for the Grill Room. It seems a shame to keep them locked up, so one day I hope to build a library at the club where they can be dis- >

Fish Cakes

SERVES 4

450 g (1 lb) white fish, smoked haddock or salmon fillet (or mixed), cut into 1 cm (½ in) cubes 30 ml (2 tablespoons) finely chopped parsley 15 ml (1 tablespoon) finely cut chives salt and freshly ground pepper	Combine in a bowl, then season with salt and pepper.
1 egg, beaten	Add, and mix to bind well. Divide the mixture into eight equal portions and roll into balls.
250 g (9 oz) potatoes peeled and roughly grated	Squeeze lightly to get rid of excess water. Place on a plate, season well, and roll the balls lightly in it to coat. Flatten the balls slightly and shape into little cakes.
15 ml (1 tablespoon) olive oil 15 g (½ oz) butter	Heat together in a pan, and shallow-fry the fish cakes gently on both sides until crisp and golden brown in colour, about 6–7 minutes. Drain well on kitchen paper.
1 lemon , cut into quarters	Serve with the fish cakes, for squeezing over them.

ANTON'S TIP

A simple parsley sauce is a good accompaniment for these fish cakes, as is braised chicory.

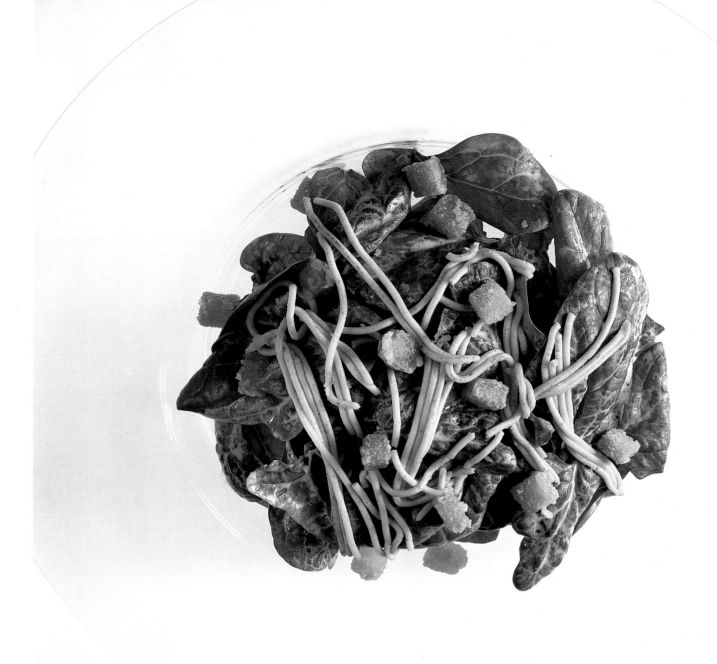

Young Spinach Leaves with Stilton

SERVES 4

400 g (14 oz) tender young spinach leaves	Pick over and wash. Drain and dry well in a salad spinner or clean cloth.
15 ml (1 tablespoon) lemon juice 5 ml (1 teaspoon) English mustard 150 g (5 oz) low-fat natural yoghurt 40 g (1½ oz) Stilton cheese, crushed with a fork salt and freshly ground pepper	Mix together until smooth, then season to taste with salt and pepper. 　Put the spinach leaves into a bowl, pour the sauce over them and toss gently to mix well. Arrange on individual plates.
100 g (4 oz) Stilton cheese, pressed into 'vermicelli' (see Tip)	Use to garnish the salads, and serve immediately.

ANTON'S TIP

To make Stilton 'vermicelli', use a mincer, a vermicelli press, the large-holed side of a grater, or push through a colander. You could of course simply cut the cheese into long thin strips.
　Roquefort and other blue cheeses could be used instead of the Stilton.

Duck Sausages with Braised Lentils

SERVES 4

500 g (18 oz) duck flesh, skinned	Very coarsely mince.
1 breast of smoked duck 100 g (4 oz) smoked bacon, rind removed	Mince together very finely.
5 ml (1 teaspoon) olive oil 100 g (4 oz) shallots, peeled and finely chopped 1 garlic clove, peeled and finely chopped	Sauté together gently to soften, then allow to cool. When cool, mix with the minced meats.
5 ml (1 teaspoon) chopped mixed herbs (parsley, thyme etc) salt and freshly ground pepper freshly grated nutmeg	Add to the mixture, seasoning to taste with salt, pepper and nutmeg.
1 egg, beaten	Add, and mix well in to bind. Place the mixture in a piping bag with a large nozzle and pipe into eight sausages of about 100 g (4 oz) each.
10 tiny sprigs rosemary 200 g (7 oz) caul fat, cut into 8 pieces	Garnish each sausage with rosemary, then wrap lightly in the caul fat. Keep cool while you prepare the duck sauce and lentils.
1 litre (1¾ pints) Brown Poultry Stock (see page 157), made with duck bones and trimmings	Reduce by boiling by about half for the duck sauce.
250 g (9 oz) brown lentils	Wash thoroughly, picking out stems and any that float. Drain well.
15 ml (1 tablespoon) olive oil 100 g (4 oz) each of potatoes and onions, peeled and finely diced 40 g (1½ oz) each of carrots and leeks, prepared and finely diced 40 g (1½ oz) tomato *concassée* (see page 35)	Sauté together in a large saucepan, for about 3–4 minutes.
600 ml (1 pint) Brown Veal Stock (see page 157) 1 small garlic clove, peeled and lightly crushed	Add, along with the drained lentils, and bring to the boil. Skim, then season with salt and pepper and simmer gently until just tender, about 20 minutes. Remove the garlic. Purée a quarter of the cooked lentils in a liquidiser then mix together with the remaining whole lentils.
10 ml (2 teaspoons) wine vinegar	Add to the braised lentils and adjust the seasoning. Keep the lentils warm while you sauté or grill the sausages for about 5–8 minutes until brown on all sides. The heat should be quite high. Divide the lentils between the serving plates and arrange two sausages on top. Serve with the duck sauce.

**Soft-selling – including my
logo on a *cappucino*!**

With Paul Bocuse at the
Cartier polo lunch at
Windsor in 1992.

MOSIMANN'S

played. For instance, I have the *Messobucco*, the first Italian cookery book ever written, but perhaps the very finest of the collection is the book written in 1605 by Bartolomeo Scappi, master chef to Pope Pius the Fifth.

The work on the club was going ahead well. The workmen were so used to seeing me around that one day when I had to fly to New York, they asked me later where I had been!

Naturally, even though my mind had been occupied with electrical wiring, plumbing and other such things, I had not forgotten about food. Quite the reverse, I was still constantly thinking of the food concept. A lot of care was also given to selecting the right plates for the food upon which so much of the presentation depended.

Then there was the wine cellar to be considered. Although we had taken on an excellent wine waiter, I was very keen to learn more about wines myself. Personally I am a great fan of champagne and port, but I am also very fond of sweet wines with a light dessert. The joys of Chi-

anti, Barolo and Frascati I discovered in Italy where on one memorable occasion we drank this fantastic bottle, full bodied and warming. It was an outstanding wine and to my amazement I discovered that it hadn't even got a label on the bottle, it was simply home-made.

Gradually everything came together and on October 1st we celebrated an official re-opening of Mosimann's, as the dining club was now officially called. Thanks to help from Lady Elizabeth Anson, Kokoly Fallah and Jean Hedley on the membership committee, within a few months we had well over a thousand members. Starting from scratch we invited individuals only, gentlemen and ladies, as the mix was very important.

The club has been a wonderful place to host all kinds of events from fund-raising in aid of the Gulf Trust or Saving the Rainforest, to wedding parties and birthday parties. Since opening our doors we have entertained royalty from over a dozen different countries, including our own, and the list of celebrities from Joan Collins, Jack Nicholson >

**The brigade responsible
for the Cartier polo lunch.
We catered for 600 people.**

In the chef's office/dining room, sponsored by Bulthaup, the German kitchen designers.

and Elizabeth Taylor to Lady Thatcher grows continually.

Since opening, the number of people asking whether we can cater for their private parties has grown so much that we started a separate party service which has been masterminded, until recently, by my wonderful assistant Kit Chan, now in Australia. It caters for anything from a quiet dinner for two to a royal banquet for over a thousand guests!

And, since the club opened, I have been busy in other ways. I was lucky enough to be asked by Yorkshire Television to do my own series. The first was called *Cooking with Mosimann*, and I was filmed preparing food for special Mosimann barbecues, breakfasts and a seven-course celebratory dinner at the club. A second series, *Anton Mosimann Naturally*, focussed on dishes without meat, and we filmed in places like Budapest, northern France, and Switzerland as well as London. Both series were accompanied by books which sold well and were a great success.

It has been an exciting, nearly five, years, with never a dull moment.

Mince Pies

MAKES APPROXIMATELY 24   OVEN: Moderately hot, 200°C/400°F/Gas 6

200 g (7 oz) plain flour a little salt	For the pastry, sift together on to a clean work surface. Make a well in the centre.
125 g (4½ oz) soft butter 75 g (3 oz) icing sugar finely grated zest of 1 lemon 1 egg, beaten	Place in the well in the flour and work together, then gradually incorporate the flour, until you have a smooth dough. Leave to rest and firm up in the fridge, covered, for at least 20 minutes. Bring out of the fridge, leave for a few minutes, then roll out on a lightly floured surface to about 3 mm (⅛ in) thick. Using a 3 cm (1¾ in) round pastry cutter, stamp out 24 rounds. Use these to line 3 cm (1¼ in) patty tins.
400 g (14 oz) mincement	Divide between the lined patty tins, filling to just over half their depth.
4 sheets filo pastry, each cut into 6 × 5cm (2in) wide strips	Take one strip, ruffle it slightly, and place over the mincemeat as a lid. Do the same to the remaining pies. Bake in the preheated oven for about 15 minutes until light golden brown. Remove from the tins using a round-bladed knife. Leave to cool a little on a wire rack.
icing sugar to dust	Serve warm with a dusting of icing sugar.

Chapter Nine

A Day in My Life

WITH THE CLUB UP AND RUNNING THERE WAS STILL NO LET-UP IN THE THINGS I HAD TO DO, BUT THEN THAT'S THE WAY I LIKE IT. THERE ARE ALWAYS NEW PARTIES TO PLAN, AND NEW MENUS TO CREATE, AND IF THERE'S ONE THING I CAN BE SURE OF, IT'S THAT I CAN NEVER BE CERTAIN WHAT THE NEXT DAY WILL BRING.

ON MOST DAYS, HOWEVER, I AM UP BY SIX-THIRTY WHEN I DRINK A CUP OF JAPANESE GREEN TEA BEFORE GOING FOR A JOG IN HOLLAND PARK. EVER SINCE I WAS YOUNG AND REGULARLY TRAINED WITH MY FATHER, I'VE LIKED TO KEEP FIT. I LIKE THE COMPETITIVE EDGE IT GIVES YOU, EVEN WHEN YOU'RE ONLY RUNNING AGAINST YOURSELF. WITH THE MIND RELAXED BY THE RHYTHM OF THE RUN, THE IDEAS FLOW, AND I'LL OFTEN THINK THINGS THROUGH WHEN I'M RUNNING. I'LL PLAN NEW PROJECTS AND SOMETIMES CREATE NEW RECIPES.

OF COURSE THE OTHER, MORE MUNDANE, REASON FOR JOGGING IS THAT I TEND TO PUT ON WEIGHT QUITE EASILY. SO FOR BREAKFAST I'LL EAT SOMETHING SATISFYING LIKE MUESLI, WHICH I SOAK THE NIGHT BEFORE. MY OTHER FAVOURITE BREAKFAST DISHES ARE FISH, SOME HADDOCK POACHED IN MILK, AND SUNDAY BRUNCH OF FRESHLY BAKED BREAD, WHICH WE HAVE WITH A SELECTION OF COLD MEATS, CHEESES, SALADS AND FRESH FRUIT.

ON WEEKDAYS, I'M IN THE OFFICE BY EIGHT-THIRTY. I SPEND AN HOUR DEALING WITH correspondence with my personal assistant, Deirdre Connor, before heading for the club. Outside stands one of our delivery vans. We bought four for our Party Service, and one is based on a classic 1930s Asquith.

Inside the Club all is quiet and the morning light streams through the stained glass. I'll walk round and say good morning to everyone before going upstairs to make a few phone calls but as often as not I'll hardly have sat down before somebody comes in with a query – about the menu for a lunch party, or to check with me how many crates of claret to buy. We keep between 12,000 and 15,000 bottles.

Next I'll run through the day's business with Eva Barkasz, the club manager (who has just won the Acorn Award), and also discuss other projects with Shelley-Anne Claircourt who deals with all the PR and marketing.

At about eleven o'clock I will put on my chef's jacket, selecting a clean one from the freshly laundered pile in the office and a bow tie from my stock in the cupboard. Then it's downstairs to the kitchen. On the way I'll walk through the bar and restaurant just to see how everything is getting on. If a picture's not straight I'll adjust it; if a waiter's got a mark on his jacket he gets told to change it. Everything has to be just right.

My *Chef de cuisine*, Ray Neve, is in charge of the day-to-day running of the kitchen, and when I get downstairs it will be to check that everything is going smoothly. In the

cold kitchen I notice that the lettuce has some brown marks on it. That's not good enough, so I tell the chef to find another. The leeks look wonderful, freshly sliced into thin green rounds.

In the hot kitchen David is preparing wild mushrooms for the fish *ragoût*. The smell is fabulous. From Thomas's bakery comes the unmistakable aroma of freshly baked rolls. We bake them ourselves, tiny fists of bread, some flavoured with saffron, others with spinach, mushroom or herbs. The selection is always changing.

I love it down here. It is my home. I still love cooking. It is relatively peaceful now, and the smells mingle and disperse throughout the kitchen but time moves on. I check the ravioli which is being filled with a subtle mixture of smoked *tofu* and herbs and served with a light basil sauce for a health award lunch. The sauce is not quite right, so I change it. Otherwise all is going well so I snatch a few minutes to make a couple of phone calls in the chef's office.

Back downstairs, the head waiter brings ten of my cookery books to sign for guests. Eva lets me know that one of our guests is celebrating their birthday today, so we arrange to prepare one of their favourite dishes.

I usually have lunch with the chefs at around midday. Fish is my favourite, grilled and served on a bed of mixed leaves. Lunch is not a long-drawn-out affair, then it's back to the kitchen.

At twelve-thirty the guests start to arrive for drinks in the bar. Downstairs the atmosphere is warming up. The sauce for the ravioli is much better now, but I think the edges of the ravioli need to be pinched more firmly together so they do not split when cooked. Everything else seems in order so it's upstairs again to greet the guests in the Wedgwood Room. I collect a starched chef's hat from the neat pile in the office and proceed upstairs. Goodness knows how many times a day I walk up and down those stairs! By the time I arrive, most of the guests have assembled and are drinking champagne. I take half a glass before joining the other judges to present the winners of the award with a trophy.

Judging is something I am often asked to do and have always enjoyed. One of the most rewarding of these occasions was when I was asked by Holloway Prison to give a demonstration at an award ceremony for a group of women prisoners who had just completed a cookery course. The delight on their faces at having achieved something worthwhile, and at being able to create good food even on a tight budget – and without a visit to the market – was unforgettable.

At ten-past one, Eva, the club manageress, motions

Lunch with Marie Helvin in the Bulthaup Room. We always have the most wonderful discussions about food, as she has been a long-standing supporter ever since we first met in Japan. She loves the oriental influence on my food.

from the door that one of the guests downstairs wants to say hello, so I make a quick detour but by one-fifteen I am back in the kitchen to ensure the safe delivery of the tuna and couscous to the Wedgwood Room. After carefully arranging each salad on its large blue or mauve glass plate, the chefs sprinkle on a dusting of paprika. The plates are now ready.

In the hot kitchen, Ray shouts out orders as they arrive from the dining room. 'Two chicken with rice. One spinach salad. Please! Quick!'

The sauce for the chicken is slightly sour. It needs a little more stock. The chicken is placed on a mound of saffron rice and chicory. The sauce, which tastes much better now, is carefully trickled on to the dish.

The chefs are multicultural, as are many of the waiters. There are exchanges in German, French, English and Italian. The mix works very well. From the pastry section comes the sweet smell of cooked apple.

Thomas, the *chef pâtissier*, calls me over to taste the carrot cake which will be served in the Wedgwood Room. It is exactly as it should be – light, delicate, not too sweet. He has decorated it with sliced almonds and a raspberry coulis.

Five minutes later five pans of ravioli are on their way upstairs where they will be freshly served from another small serving kitchen next to the dining-room. The sauce now needs a touch more pepper . . .

At one-forty the ravioli is served and the trolley is sent down for the main course, steamed haddock served with a courgette and fennel compote. The fish has been steamed for just a couple of minutes and the flesh glistens, firm and white. After they have finished eating I will go upstairs to check that they are all happy .

During service, the pace is hectic but by two-thirty I have time to interview a student looking for a work placement. Clare seems enterprising and bright, so I offer her

Mushroom hunting in Kent with the kitchen brigade, and a friend, Victoria Sharp.

the job of putting my collection of recipes on to computer. It will take her some time; I have eight cabinets filled with recipes I have collected from all over the world.

Every so often one of the chefs comes in with a query, then a friend arrives from Canada, a chef I met at the Queen Elizabeth whom I haven't seen for five or six years. He has dropped in with his son, so they stay for coffee. Clare stays too, looking rather bemused. This is not your usual kind of job interview, but then if I like somebody and see potential in them, I like to treat them as a friend, as part of the family.

At around three-thirty, I take a couple of hours' break to swim or work out in the gym, but by six o'clock at the latest I'm back at the club and will often fit in a meeting before going down to the kitchen.

The meeting might be about a new product. Recently I have been discussing with designers the packaging of a new range of Mosimann chocolates which I hope will be as popular as our Christmas puddings of which we sold 25,000 in the first year alone!

Or it might be about the Party Service, which is busy this weekend with several large functions. Undoubtedly the greatest challenge we have ever taken on was to prepare a banquet for the Duke of Edinburgh.

That started with a simple enough request. 'Would you like to cook dinner for Prince Philip's seventieth birthday party?' I was asked by Countess Alexander of Tunis, a special events consultant.

'Of course I'd love to,' I said. 'It would be a pleasure.'

'There will be 1,400 guests,' she said.

The banquet was intended to raise funds for the Duke's favourite charities, and in particular the thirty-fifth anniversary of the Duke of Edinburgh Award, and was being held in giant marquees in the grounds of Windsor Castle.

Obviously I was going to need some experienced help so I started to phone friends and colleagues. One of those first calls was to Albert Schnell in Montreal, the man who had first shown me how to organise a banquet all those years ago. Two friends who ran restaurants in Zürich – Rosa Tschudi and Heinz Witschi – came as well. I also rang old colleagues from the Dorchester and chefs who had once trained with me and were now working as head chefs all over the country. In all I gathered together a team of fifty strong who were to be overseen by Kit.

THE JOY OF MY WORK COMES FROM BEING ABLE TO COOK FOR PEOPLE I KNOW, TO I

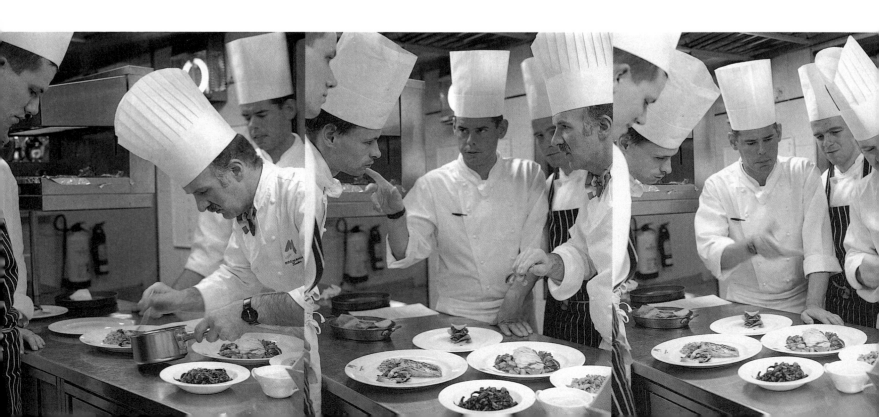

Together we sat down to plan the menu. We all agreed it should be a cold meal, as the banquet was being held at the end of July. To start we would serve a mixture of grilled and marinated summer vegetables – courgettes, peppers, baby corn and cherry tomatoes. This would be followed by a light cream herb soup, maize-fed chicken with turmeric and couscous, followed by bread and butter pudding, served with raspberry coulis flavoured with *Framboise* liqueur. Then finally a selection of cheeses, a Roalp and *Tête de Moine* (monk's head) and an English farmhouse Cheddar served with warm walnut bread.

As well as preparing the food, we needed to find 300 waiters and waitresses to serve it. Where on earth were we going to find such a vast number? After some thought we came up with the good solution of approaching students at a number of local catering colleges. They agreed to help, and with the aid of a training video we talked through the table settings and logistics until we were confident they would sail through on the night. Which of course, after a few hours of rehearsal on the day, they did!

When we drove to Windsor to organise the setting-up of the catering tents behind the main marquee, I was astonished by the sight before my eyes. It was magnificent, like being transported back in time. The imposing dark stone battlements, the expanse of grass, the great marquees gathered about with ropes, and people all around looked as if these were elaborate preparations for some magnificent medieval tournament.

The kitchens consisted of two marquees leading directly on to the main dining-room, in the largest marquee of all. Behind the kitchens stood six walk-in refrigerators each manned by eight chefs. Attached to each team were fifty waiters who in turn served 250 guests!

It was an extraordinary evening, particularly for the chefs and other staff who had started serious work at lunchtime on Friday and worked through, virtually without break, until two or three o'clock on Saturday morning.

Before dinner the guests were served champagne and canapés, which we prepared at the very last moment. The waiters and waitresses carried around hundreds of salvers of *sushi*, carrot mousse on tiny muffins and spicy prawns in tartlets, as well as marinated and barbecued tuna and cream cheese with chives, on bread rounds.

Then came the moment we had all been waiting for as >

TO GIVE THEM THEIR FAVOURITE DISHES OR COOK SOMETHING THEY RARELY HAVE.

I SOUGHT TO CREATE A CUISINE DEDICATED TO

COMBINING THE IDEALS OF 'GOOD FOOD' AND 'FOOD

THAT IS GOOD FOR YOU', TWO THINGS THAT HAD

UNTIL NOW SEEMED MUTUALLY EXCLUSIVE . . .

I WAS DETERMINED TO CREATE A HAPPY BALANCE, A CUISINE WHICH

OFFERED MOUTH–WATERING RECIPES THAT WERE NOT LADEN

WITH SALT, SUGAR AND FAT YET PROVIDED THE FRESH FRUIT, VEGETABLES, PRO

the guests slowed moved to the tables. There was no time now for mistakes, but thankfully we had no need to worry. With so many courageous hands involved, the evening went off brilliantly, coming to a climax with the appearance of a splendid four-foot-high celebration cake.

On more ordinary evenings at the club, however, once the meetings are over, I will check through any last-minute messages before putting on my white jacket to go down to the kitchen. Here I will run through the function sheets with Ray. Tonight we have fifty covers in the Harvey Nichols room, twenty-one in the Wedgwood, twelve in the Gucci, eight in the Alfa Romeo, and the restaurant is full. It will be a busy night and I want to ensure that everything is ready.

The *mise en place* – finely chopped onion, tomatoes and other ingredients necessary for the making of sauces – are all prepared so that the sauces can be cooked freshly at the last minute. In the *garde-manger* I taste everything. The salmon terrine, spicy noodles, the smoked trout and the dressings. The tuna *tataki,* seared earlier, has now cooled and tastes delicious, just a hint of smoke on the outside. A clean spoon to taste the herb sauce . . . very good.

There's no time to stop, I go straight to the pastry section where Ray scoops out a little of the cinnamon ice cream for me to taste. This will be served with chocolate and pecan pie. It is good, as is the blackcurrant sorbet.

At seven-thirty I go upstairs to check on the progress of the canapés service. It seems fine, so I head straight back downstairs where four heads are bent over, concentrating on the preparation of the saddle of rabbit Provençale. It will take some trial and error to decide on the best arrangement of each new dish.

I'm not happy with the way the rabbit has been cut. It would look better to leave the saddle whole, rather than cut into slices. I demonstrate the cut I'm after and ask the chef to carry on as I have shown him.

Meanwhile at the back of the kitchen some oxtails are >

AND DIETARY FIBRE SO OFTEN LACKING IN A WESTERN DIET.

A special corner in the club!

being simmered gently in large pans for several hours. They will then cool overnight and the fat will be scraped off the top in the morning.

At seven-forty I have a light meal of grilled halibut with Ray, and we discuss last-minute changes to the menu. Often Eva joins us as well.

Back in the kitchen, the first orders have started coming in 'One home-smoked rainbow trout! Two guinea fowl! One seafood tagliatelle!'

Each chef responds to the order independently and almost imperceptibly. I stir the sauce, check the vegetables and once I am certain that all is well, I dash into the *garde-manger* to see how the Caesar salad is going. I rearrange the leaves slightly then, back in the kitchen, I taste the risotto.

The pace is hotting up now. Orders are coming in from the restaurant every two minutes, and at the same time we have to send fifty plates of lamb with herb sauce to the Harvey Nichols room.

The lamb is ready but we are waiting for the sauce. This now appears. The vegetables, potatoes, leek with carrot and red cabbage are ready. The temperature has risen, the tempo too. Everything must be assembled, all with the same care and attention, even when the pressure is on. With practice nobody need lose their cool even under the severest conditions. And finally, we are ready and the waiters take the dishes upstairs to the servery where the food is plated.

I take a quick moment in the chef's dining-room, before four booked-in guests arrive, so that I can run through an Indonesian dinner for fifty which is being planned for next week. Another guest is organising a party for seventy: he selects spicy prawns with salad, risotto with wild mushrooms, fillet of lamb with herb sauce, and bread and butter pudding. That all seems fine, so I leave Eva to sort out the final arrangements and head back to the kitchen. With so much to do, my assistants are very much appreciated.

Eight forty-five and the orders are flooding in.

'Two poached halibut. Two risotti. Three Hoisin baby chicken. Let's go!'

'Two tuna *tataki,* two steak *tartare!*'

Ray calls out the order. He doesn't need to shout although this is the busiest moment. I like to keep the noise to a decent level in the kitchen, otherwise before you know it, everyone is yelling and no-one can hear.

Minutes later the halibut is cooked and carefully arranged on salad leaves.

'The steak *tartare, c'est prêt?*' asks the waiter.

In the pastry kitchen fifty black plates are being decorated with toasted silvers of almond ready for the chocolate and pecan pie with ice cream.

The pace keeps up for an hour or so as we work through the orders. By ten-thirty things begin to calm down and unless we have a large party, going on late into the night, I should be leaving by eleven. Sometimes, though, I will be there till the early hours of the morning. It's all part of this wonderful business that I love, and that is such an important element of my life.

I FEEL LIKE A PROUD FATHER WHOSE CHILDREN HAVE GONE OUT AND NOW HOI

A happy moment in the
Gucci Room after lunch,
just before an interview.

IMPORTANT POSITIONS IN SOME OF THE BEST KITCHENS IN THE WORLD.

BASIC RECIPES

There are just a few basics needed for the recipes throughout the book. The stocks are the most important, as a good stock adds immeasurably to the flavour of a soup or sauce, or indeed any dish. The other two recipes can be used in many different ways.

Vegetable Stock

MAKES ABOUT 1 LITRE (1¾ PINTS)

40 g (1½ oz) each of onion and leek 20 g (¾ oz) each of celery and fennel 30 g (1¼ oz) each of cabbage and tomato	Peel, trim, wash, etc as appropriate, cut up and chop finely. Keep them separate.
30 ml (2 tablespoons) vegetable oil	Heat in a large pan and sweat the onion and leek in it for 4–5 minutes. Add the remaining vegetables and sweat for a further 10 minutes.
1.2 litres (2 pints) cold water ½ bay leaf 1 clove	Add, and simmer for 20 minutes. Strain through a fine sieve or cloth, allowing it to drip.
salt and freshly ground pepper	Season to taste with salt and pepper. Use immediately, or refrigerate for a short time, or freeze in small containers.

White Poultry or Veal Stock

MAKES 1 LITRE (1¾ PINTS)

1 kg (2¼ lb) raw poultry pieces or veal bones, finely chopped 2 litres (3½ pints) water	Place together in a saucepan, and bring to the boil. Skim.
50 g (2 oz) white bouquet garni (onion, white of leek, celeriac or celery, and herbs) tied together salt and freshly ground pepper	Add, and season lightly. Leave to simmer carefully for 2 hours, covered, occasionally skimming and removing the fat. Strain through a fine cloth or sieve, allowing it to drip, and season to taste.

ANTON'S TIP

For the poultry stock, you could use a boiling fowl, but blanch it first in boiling water. You could use the flesh afterwards for various cold dishes.

   Calves feet and/or veal trimmings may be added to, or used instead of, the veal bones.

Fish Stock

MAKES ABOUT 1 LITRE (1¾ PINTS)

900 g (2 lb) white fish bones and trimmings	Wash thoroughly and chop up finely.
30 ml (2 tablespoons) vegetable oil 60 g (2½ oz) mirepoix (peeled, diced onion, white of leek, celeriac, fennel leaves and dill) 30 g (1¼ oz) mushroom trimmings	Sweat together in a suitable pan until the vegetables have softened.
1.2 litres (2 pints) cold water 60 ml (4 tablespoons) white wine	Add, along with the fish bones and trimmings, and simmer for 20 minutes, occasionally skimming and removing any fat. Strain through a fine sieve or a cloth.
salt and freshly ground pepper	Season to taste with salt and pepper. Use immediately, keep in the refrigerator for a short time, or freeze in small containers.

Brown Poultry or Veal Stock

MAKES 1 LITRE (1¾ PINTS)   OVEN: Moderate, 180°C/350°F/Gas 4

1 kg (2¼ lb) raw poultry or veal bones and trimmings, cut in small pieces 20 ml (¾ fl oz) vegetable oil	Place in a roasting tin and brown in the oven on all sides for about 30–40 minutes. Strain off all the fat.
50 g (2 oz) *mirepoix* (peeled, diced onion, carrot, celeriac or celery, and herbs) 100 g (4 oz) tomatoes, diced	Add and continue to roast carefully for a further 4–5 minutes. Remove the tin from the oven and transfer its contents to a large saucepan.

2 litres (3½ pints) water, or (preferably) the appropriate White Stock (opposite)	First add 500 ml (17 fl oz), bring to the boil, then boil to reduce to a glaze.
	   Add the same amount of water again and reduce to a glaze.
	   Add the remaining water and simmer carefully for 2 hours, occasionally skimming and removing the fat.

salt and freshly ground pepper	Strain through a cloth or fine sieve, allowing it to drip, and season to taste.

ANTON'S TIP

The veal stock can benefit in taste from the addition of up to 500 g (18 oz) tomatoes. If you like, you can add 300 ml (10 fl oz) dry white wine to the first water or stock quantity.
   Make brown lamb etc stocks in the same way, substituting lamb bones for the poultry or veal.

Vanilla Cream

SERVES 4

250 ml (8 fl oz) milk ½ vanilla pod	Bring to the boil together in a saucepan.

3 egg yolks
80 g (3¼ oz) caster sugar
40 g (1½ oz) plain flour
	Mix together in a bowl. Add the boiling milk and mix well.
	   Return the mixture to the saucepan and bring to the boil slowly. Continue to boil for 2–3 minutes, stirring constantly.
	   Strain through a fine sieve and serve warm or cold.

7.5 ml (½ tablespoon) caster sugar (optional)	Sprinkle over the cream if it is to be served cold, to prevent a skin forming.

Meringue

SERVES 4

2 egg whites	Place in a clean wide bowl and whisk until soft peaks form.
50 g (2 oz) caster sugar	Add gradually, whisking continuously, until the mix is a stiff snow. Use immediately.

ANTON'S TIP

This mix can also be used for tea-time and *petits-fours* meringues. Bake in a very low oven until dry.

Index

Page numbers in *italic* refer to illustrations

Recipes are in **bold**

Acknowledgements

My sincere thanks to the kitchen brigade for all their support particularly to Ray Neve and Georg Heise.

Special thanks also go to Shelley-Anne Claircourt, Deirdre Connor and Eva Barkasz.

The publishers would like to thank the Dorchester for use of the photograph of The Grill Room, on page 101.